Voltaire

ff

VOLTAIRE

A. J. Ayer

faber and faber

LONDON · BOSTON

First published in Great Britain in 1986 by
George Weidenfeld and Nicholson Limited, London
This paperback edition first published in 1988 by
Faber and Faber Limited
3 Queen Square London WC1N 3AU

Printed in Great Britain by
Cox & Wyman Ltd
All rights reserved

British Library Cataloguing in Publication Data

Ayer, A. J.
Voltaire.
1. Voltaire——Criticism and
interpretation
I. Title
848′.509   PQ2099

ISBN 0-571-15024-1

In memory of Vanessa

Contents

Preface

Voltaire's fame is undiminished but I suspect that very little of his work is now much read, apart from *Candide* and to a lesser extent the *Pocket Philosophical Dictionary*. I have made not an exhaustive but a serious attempt to remedy this deficiency. After a succinct account of Voltaire's life and character, I briefly assess his skill as a dramatist and historian, his involvement in religious, scientific and philosophical controversy, and the nature of his philosophical thought. While I acknowledge how much of his time and energy was spent in denouncing and endeavouring to redress the abuses of Christianity, I stress the fact that he was not an atheist but a deist, and I try to show that his deism raised theoretical problems which he was unable to resolve. This does not detract from my admiration of his moral courage.

Especially in my first chapter I have largely relied on the biographies of Voltaire written respectively by Theodore Besterman and Jean Orieux. I am indebted also to Professor Robert Shackleton of All Souls College, Oxford, for drawing my attention to Fréderic Lachèvre's *Voltaire mourant*, from which I have taken my account of Voltaire's last days.

Except where I explicitly state otherwise, the translations from the French are my own.

As so often before, I owe thanks to Mrs Guida Crowley for typing my manuscript and assisting me in checking the index. I wish also to thank Mr Benjamin Buchan at Weidenfeld for his help in seeing the work through the press.

A. J. Ayer
51 York Street, London W. 1
September 1985

I

Life and Character

François-Marie Arouet, who became famous under the name of Voltaire, was baptized in Paris at the church of Saint-André-des-Arcs on 22 November 1694, most probably on the day following his birth. He himself was apt to say in later life that he was born on 20 February 1694 at the Arouets' country house at Châtenay a few miles outside Paris, but he liked to indulge in mystification, and there is no evidence to support this claim, which is contradicted by extant copies of his certificate of baptism. He was also disposed to proclaim himself illegitimate, hinting that he was the son of a song-writer called Rochebrune, but this too was almost certainly a pretence, fostered perhaps by his disdain for his actual father, François Arouet, a respectable notary who by 1692 had made his way into the college of heraldry as a collector of spice taxes in the Royal Exchequer, a lucrative as well as an honourable office.

The Arouet family had gradually made its way up from being artisans in Poitou. François Arouet, who was born in 1650, was the seventh child of a cloth-merchant who had set up shop in Paris. In 1683 he married Marie-Marguerite Daumart who came from a rather better family, her father being a clerk to the Paris *parlement*, the most important of the French law-courts. They had six children of whom three died in infancy. The other two who survived were Voltaire's elder brother Armand, born in 1685, who pursued the same career as his father, but differed from him and still more from Voltaire in being a religious fanatic, and an elder sister, named Marguerite after her mother and born in 1690. At the age of eighteen she married Pierre-François Mignot, a supervisor at the Royal Exchequer and bore him two daughters Marie-Louise in 1712 and Marie-Elisabeth in 1724. Little is known of Voltaire's mother who died when he was in his seventh year and his family affections were concentrated on his sister and her children.

When he was nine years old, François-Marie Arouet, as he was still called, was sent as a boarder to the Jesuit College of Louis-Le-Grand in Paris, where he remained for seven years. He received a classical education, principally in Latin with a smattering of Greek. He was taught French literature and composition, French and classical history, the rudiments of mathematics but no science. Neither did the Jesuits overburden their charges with theology. Young Arouet was a good, if not especially devout pupil, chiefly conspicuous for his precocious skill in composing French verses. The school attracted pupils from the nobility and several of them, notably the future Duc de Richelieu, who won fame as a soldier, the brothers Marquis d'Argenson and Comte d'Argenson, who respectively served as minister for foreign affairs and minister for war, and Comte d'Argental, who became a lawyer, formed friendships with Arouet which persisted into later life. For all the hostility which Arouet, in the persona of Voltaire, came to display towards Christianity, he retained an affectionate memory of his Jesuit teachers, especially his prefect Father d'Olivet and his teacher of rhetoric Father Porée.

François-Marie was only twelve when his godfather, the irreligious Abbé de Châteauneuf, took him to visit Ninon de l'Enclos. The famous courtesan, then in her eighties, was so impressed by the boy that she bequeathed him two thousand francs with which to buy books. It can only have been a year or two later that the Abbé, who died in 1708, introduced his godson into the Society of the Temple, the headquarters of a group of libertines and free-thinkers, including the Duc de Sully and the poets La Fare and Chaulieu. Their leader, Philippe de Bourbon-Vendôme, Grand Prior of the Knights of St John of Jerusalem, and an illegitimate grandson of Henri IV, had been exiled by Louis XIV, under the influence of Madame de Maintenon, and it was not until the king's death in 1715 that he was able to resume his position.

Meanwhile François-Marie Arouet had established himself in this company, attracting notice as a wit and a dandy and, after leaving college, so far from proceeding to the study of the law, as his father wished, declared his intention of becoming a man of letters. In 1712 he competed for a prize offered by the French Academy for an ode to the Virgin Mary, in fulfilment of a vow made by Louis XIII. He had no doubt that his entry deserved the prize, but it was awarded to the Abbé Dujarry. This setback did nothing to modify his way of life which so displeased his father that he banished him first to Caen and then to The Hague where the Marquis de Châteauneuf was French Ambassador and was willing to attach the young Arouet at least nominally to his staff.

There was a colony of French Huguenots at The Hague, among them a Madame Dunoyer, a lady of bad reputation, with two daughters for whom she was seeking husbands. The younger daughter was called Olympe and nicknamed Pimpette. She was quick to succumb to Arouet, as she addressed him in her wildly ungrammatical letters, and he returned her love to the point of begging her to elope with him. Learning of this, Madame Dunoyer complained to the French Ambassador who sent his new attaché back in disgrace to Paris. After a period of pining for her lover, Pimpette allowed herself to bestow her hand upon a man with sounder prospects, of whom her mother could approve.

François-Marie, a highly jealous man in the world of letters but not in love, continued to hold Pimpette in affection, but his most immediate concern was the anger of his father who went so far as to apply for a *lettre de cachet* authorizing him to send his son to prison or exile him to the West Indies. He was placated by his son's consenting to be articled to a lawyer, Maître Alain. François-Marie endured this for a few months, forming a lasting friendship with a fellow-clerk Nicolas Thieriot and publishing two satirical poems *Le Bourbier* (The Mire) and *L'Anti-Giton*, addressed to a homosexual. *L'Anti-Giton* was dedicated to Mlle Duclos who became

3

a leading actress at the Comédie-Française under the name of Adrienne Lecouvreur. François-Marie made a profession of love to Mlle Duclos but was rejected in favour of the Comte d'Uzès. He consoled himself with the Marquise de Mimeure.

Observing that his son was not seriously studying the law, François Arouet again threatened to have him punished. The young man was rescued by an old friend of the family, the Marquis de Caumartin, who had him to stay at his country house near Fontainebleau. The Marquis was a first-hand authority on seventeenth-century France and supplied his guest with some of the material which he incorporated thirty-six years later into one of his historical works, *Le Siècle de Louis XIV*. By this early date François-Marie had already composed *Oedipe*, the first of his tragedies in verse, and was hoping to arrange for its performance.

When the long reign of Louis XIV came to an end in 1715, his great-grandson who succeeded him as Louis XV was only five years old. There was accordingly a regency, entrusted to Louis XIV's nephew Philippe d'Orléans who instituted a far more liberal regime. François-Marie Arouet took advantage of this to return to Paris and was still further emboldened to circulate a poem implying that the Regent was committing incest with his daughter, the Duchesse de Berry. Whatever the facts, the publication of the poem was thought to be going too far and its author was banished to Tulle. At the request of his father, who uncharacteristically intervened in his favour, his place of exile was changed to Sully-sur-Loire, where he became a guest of his friend the Duke and started a love affair with a young actress, Suzanne de Livry.

At the instigation of Chaulieu, his friend from the Temple, he wrote an epistle in verse to the Regent, disclaiming his authorship of the offending poem, and was allowed to return to Paris in October 1716. After remaining quiet for over six months he was accused of circulating two more poems, each highly defamatory of the government. He had in fact written only one of them but it was enough to cause the Regent to sentence him to prison. He entered the Bastille in May 1717 and remained there for eleven months.

It was during this period that François-Marie Arouet assumed the surname of Voltaire. The provenance of the name is uncertain, the most commonly held opinion being that it was a rough anagram of Arouet L. J., short for Arouet Le Jeune, with the 'u' transformed into a 'v' and the 'j' into an 'i'. The earliest extant letter to carry the new name is dated June 1718, two months after the author's release from prison. It is addressed to the Earl of Ashburnham, asking for the loan of a horse, and signed Arouet de Voltaire. Subsequently the Arouet was simply dropped. There appears to be no accounting for the honorific particle which Voltaire assumed.

The conditions of imprisonment in the Bastille at that time were not onerous, at any rate for someone like Voltaire. He was allowed visitors and books and the leisure to write. He devoted himself mainly to composing his epic poem on the rise to power of Henri IV, the first Bourbon king of France, who reigned from 1589 to 1610. To secure his power, Henri de Navarre, as he then was, had to allow himself to be converted from Protestantism to Catholicism in 1593 with his well-known remark that Paris was worth a mass. His greatest achievement was the proclamation of the Edict of Nantes in 1598 which secured toleration for the Huguenots and their Protestantism, until the edict was revoked in 1685 by Louis XIV. Voltaire's poem, which was eventually entitled *La Henriade* and ran to ten laborious cantos, concentrated on the religious conflict, amounting to civil war, which preceded and attended Henri's access to power. For this reason, the poem was originally entitled *La Ligue*, with reference to the Catholic party, organized by the Guise family, which led the opposition to Henri of Navarre. It was under this title that it was first published in Geneva in 1723 and again in Amsterdam in 1724. The change of title to *La Henriade* first occurred in a London edition of 1728, reprinted in Paris, though ostensibly again in London, in 1730, and officially in Paris in 1731, with fifteen other French editions to follow. The delay over its official publication in France resulted from the suspicion that parts of it reflected adversely on the government of Louis XV, who was emancipated from the Regency in 1723. Here the fifth canto in which Voltaire rebukes Fanaticism may have played a part. There is one line in which he is mildly derisive of the Eucharist, speaking of the communicant as having the priest discover a God for him in the form of a piece of bread which no longer exists.

What may be the best portrait of Voltaire was painted by Nicolas Largillière in 1718, probably after Voltaire's release from prison. I shall not try to improve on Theodore Besterman's description of the portrait, which he acquired as part of his vast collection of objects and manuscripts appertaining to Voltaire.

> The eyes are a brilliant brown; the nose is long, and slightly bulbous; the mouth is large, sensitive, smiling; the face thin, already showing the lines of humour and, perhaps, of bad health; the whole is crowned by a very high forehead, and framed by a full, unusually long, loose, pale wig; a red and buff waistcoat is elegantly unbuttoned at top and bottom to show the handsome shirt and lace jabot; the coat is of dark emerald velvet, with large gold buttons.[1]

In all, one is left with no doubt of Voltaire's intelligence, his addiction to mischief and his self-assurance.

It appears that there were three versions of this portrait, one of which Voltaire gave to Suzanne de Livry, though he knew of her infidelity to him with his friend Génonville, with whom he was quite content to share her. Génonville was a young lawyer whose early death in the smallpox epidemic of 1723 greatly distressed Voltaire. Ten years later Voltaire wrote a verse epistle to his shade in which he spoke of the loss to himself as still dreadful and new. With Suzanne de Livry he remained on good terms, to the point of insisting on her playing Jocasta in his *Oedipe*, a part to which we are told that her talents were unequal. Presumably she returned his affection, though she described him as a chilly lover, 'un amant à la neige'.

Oedipe, the earliest of Voltaire's numerous verse tragedies, was first performed at the Comédie-Française on 18 November 1718, at a date when Voltaire, though released from the Bastille, had obtained only provisional leave to reside in Paris; his full liberty was not restored to him until the following April. The play was

---

[1]Theodore Besterman, *Voltaire*, p. 81.

an immediate success, achieving forty-five performances, an exceptional number for those days. Voltaire received a gold medal and a pension from the Regent: he was hailed as the equal of Racine and Corneille. He himself thought his play superior to the *Oedipus Tyrannus* of Sophocles, partly on the curious ground that it withholds the secret of Oedipus's parentage from the audience until the dénouement, whereas in Sophocles's version the audience is made party to the secret almost from the beginning and the dramatic effect is obtained by its gradual revelation to the characters in the play and finally to Oedipus himself. Voltaire, perhaps under pressure from the management of the Comédie-Française, thought it necessary to introduce a love-interest and so brought Philoctetes, the famous archer and protégé of Hercules, into a legend in which he had no place, making him the lover of the youthful Jocasta, whom she secretly continued to prefer to Laius, and to Laius's and her son Oedipus, whom she had successively found herself required to marry. This considerably affects the character of the story but can hardly be said to add to its power.

It would seem that the popularity of the play was due to some extent to its being thought to be covertly subversive. For instance, Philoctetes is made to say that whereas a king is revered as a god by his subjects, he and Hercules regard him as an ordinary man. There is also a rather more daring couplet in which it is proclaimed that our priests are not what a foolish people think; the whole of their science consists in our credulity. These verses are said to have been greeted with applause.

Voltaire was encouraged by the success of *Oedipe* to persuade the Comédie-Française to produce his *Artémire* in February 1720. It resembled *Oedipe* in being set in ancient Greece but met with a very different reception, so hostile indeed that the play was withdrawn after its first performance. Voltaire rewrote it but it fared no better in its revised than in its original form. Thereafter he abandoned it and never allowed it to be published.

In the next few years Voltaire divided his time between publishing *La Henriade*, declaiming parts of it in various country houses, and making money out of investment and speculation. On the advice of his bankers, the brothers Paris, he did particularly well out of the collapse of John Law's 'system'. John Law was a Scotsman whom the Regent had made Comptroller General of Finance and the basis of his system was the substitution of paper money for gold. The experiment failed because of the excessive confidence, leading to wild speculation, which it aroused. Curiously, its failure occurred in the same year, 1720, as the pricking of the South Sea Bubble in England.

In this year, in which he embarked on his career as a man of business, which he was never to forsake, Voltaire narrowly escaped assassination at the hands of a police spy, Captain Beauregard, whose testimony had helped to cause his imprisonment three years earlier. With some difficulty Voltaire obtained a warrant for Beauregard's arrest but Beauregard was protected by the minister of war, Monsieur Le Blanc, and it was not until Le Blanc was replaced by Voltaire's friend the Baron de Breteuil two years later that Beauregard was lodged in prison. His eventual fate is not known.

In 1722 Voltaire's father died, leaving Voltaire only a third of his residual estate in trust. The major part of his considerable fortune went to Armand, to whom just before his death he transferred his lucrative post at the Exchequer. Little as he approved of Armand's religious fervour he preferred it to François-Marie's free thinking and free living. Voltaire contested the will unsuccessfully but had no reason to be downcast. The Regent increased his pension and when combined with his heritage and the profits from his own financial dealings, this set him well on the road to becoming a rich man.

Within a year of his father's death, Voltaire visited Flanders in the company of the Marquise de Rumpelmonde, a widow rather older than himself. She inspired him to compose a long poem entitled *Épître à Uranie* or *Le Pour et Le Contre*, in which he made a forthright attack on all forms of Christianity. Voltaire kept the poem by him for another ten years and then allowed it to circulate only privately. It did not appear in an official edition of his works until 1772. Otherwise the main fruit of this excursion was his falling-out with the poet Jean-Baptiste (not to be confused with Jean-Jacques) Rousseau, who was living in exile in Brussels. They began with a great show of friendship, but Voltaire seems to have given offence to the older poet by decrying his work. Rousseau responded by affecting to be greatly shocked by the *Épître à Uranie*, which Voltaire had shown him, and by denouncing Voltaire and Madame de Rumpelmonde as a disreputable couple. Voltaire waited seventeen years for his revenge. When he again visited Brussels in 1739, and Rousseau showed him a very long poem entitled 'Ode to Posterity', he commented 'I doubt if this ode will ever reach its destination'.

The smallpox epidemic to which his friend Génonville succumbed was very nearly fatal to Voltaire. He was saved by the skill of his physician Monsieur de Gervasi and the attentions both of his hosts, the President and Madame de Maisons, and his friend Thieriot who remained with him throughout his illness. Meanwhile Voltaire's epic poem, still called *La Ligue*, was circulating secretly in Paris and was much admired. For anyone who has the stamina to read the whole of it today it is as hard to understand why it was thought worthy of such admiration as why the French authorities were at all concerned to suppress it.

Adrienne Lecouvreur, who also had visited Voltaire during his illness, was given the leading part in his tragedy *Mariamne*, which was produced at the Comédie-Française in March 1724. It was again a failure. The plot required Mariamne, the heroine, to be poisoned by Herod and the public thought it indecorous that she was made to expire upon the stage. After Voltaire cut out this scene in his revision of the play, it was quite well received. At about the same time, he wrote a curtain-raiser *L'Indiscret*, which seems to me to owe something to Congreve's *Love for Love*, though it is a very much slighter work.

By 1725 Voltaire had succeeded in finding favour at court. He achieved this by making friends with Madame de Prie, the mistress of the Duc de Bourbon who was then Prime Minister and exercised a strong influence over the young King Louis XV. Voltaire was invited to the marriage of the King to Marie Lesczynska. The young queen was moved to tears when she read *Mariamne* and increased his pension.

Voltaire's social pretensions received a rude shock at the end of the year. There are various accounts of the incident, which differ in detail though not in any essential point. I quote Lytton Strachey's version.

> One night at the Opéra the Chevalier de Rohan-Chabot, of the famous and powerful family of the Rohans, a man of forty-three, quarrelsome, blustering, whose reputation for courage left something to be desired, began to taunt the poet upon his birth – 'Monsieur Arouet, Monsieur Voltaire – what *is* your name?' To which the retort came quickly – 'Whatever my name may be, I know how to preserve the honour of it'. The Chevalier muttered something and went off, but the incident was not ended ... A few days later Voltaire and the Chevalier met again, at the Comédie, in Adrienne Lecouvreur's dressing-room. Rohan repeated his sneering question and 'the Chevalier has had his answer' was Voltaire's reply. Furious, Rohan lifted his stick, but at that moment Adrienne very properly fainted, and the company dispersed.[1]

Not long afterwards Voltaire was dining at the town house of his friend the Duc de Sully when he was told that a messenger wanted to speak with him. He went out into the street and was immediately seized and beaten by a gang of ruffians. The Chevalier, who had employed them, called out from his carriage 'Spare his head. It is still fit to entertain the public', causing some bystanders to exclaim at his kindness. Voltaire rushed back to the dinner party, complaining volubly of the ill-treatment which he had received, but his host and the other guests listened to him with cold indifference. He had the mortification of measuring the shallowness of their friendship. They found him good company, but were not ready to take his part against a member of a noble family. Voltaire could only repay the treachery of the Duc de Sully by removing all mention of his ancestor, the friend and minister of Henri IV, from *La Henriade*.

He hoped to revenge himself more effectively upon the Chevalier de Rohan-Chabot. After appealing in vain for sympathy from the

[1]Lytton Strachey, *Books and Characters* (London, 1934), 'Voltaire and England', pp. 94–5.

Abbé de Caumartin and for redress from the Duc d'Orléans and
Madame de Prie, he went into hiding on the outskirts of Paris,
and took lessons in fencing with the intention of challenging the
Chevalier to a duel and killing him. When this became known to
the Rohan family they obtained from the Duc de Bourbon a warrant
for Voltaire's arrest. He was discovered by the police and on 17
April 1726 re-entered the Bastille. This caused the tide of public
opinion to turn in his favour and he received many visitors. Consequently, when he expressed a wish to visit England, the authorities
were pleased to grant it. He was released from the Bastille on 11
May and at once made his way to Calais.

Voltaire was not ill-equipped for a sojourn in England. He had
a letter of recommendation from the foreign secretary, the Comte
de Morville, to the Comte de Broglie, the French Ambassador to
the court of St James, he was a good friend of Lord Bolingbroke
who had returned to England after living in France since 1717 with
the Marquise de Villette who became his second wife, and he had
adequate bills of exchange drawn upon a Portuguese Jewish broker
called Medina. However, when he reached London in July, appar-
ently after returning secretly to France in another vain attempt to
confront and fight the Chevalier de Rohan-Chabot, he discovered,
as he put it in a letter written in English to Thieriot, that 'my
damned Jew was broken'. 'I was', the letter continues, 'without
a penny, sick to death of a violent agüe, a stranger, alone, helpless,
in the midst of a city, wherein I was known to no body. My Lord
and Lady Bolingbroke were in the country. I could not make bold
to see our ambassador in so wretched a condition. I had never under-
gone such distress; but I am born to run through all the misfortunes
of life.'

He was rescued from this plight by 'a single gentleman', a merchant called Everard Falkener, who had met Voltaire once in Paris,
and now installed him in his country house at Wandsworth. Apart
from his generosity, Falkener must have had unusual qualities, since
he went on to become the first English Ambassador at Constantinople, then Postmaster-General, and wound up, in Lytton Strachey's
terms, 'by marrying ... at the age of sixty-three, the illegitimate

daughter of General Churchill'.[1] Otherwise, nothing is known of him.

Once he had recovered his spirits Voltaire made his presence known to the Bolingbrokes who received him warmly and introduced him to their friends. He met Pope and Swift and Gay, who showed him a copy of *The Beggar's Opera* before it was acted. He attended Newton's funeral, discussed metaphysics with Samuel Clarke, and Milton's *Paradise Lost* with the poet Edward Young, eliciting the couplet

> You are so witty profligate and thin
> At once we think you Satan, Death and Sin.

He called upon Congreve who affected surprise at such attention being paid to an ordinary English gentleman. 'If you were only a gentleman,' said Voltaire, 'I should not have had the honour of being here today.' Voltaire very quickly mastered the English language. There is a well-known story of his being set upon by a crowd in a London street, abusing him as a 'French dog', his leaping upon a milestone, and turning their jeers to applause with a speech beginning 'Good Englishmen! Am I not already unfortunate enough in not having been born among you?' He actually published two essays in English, one on the French Civil Wars and another on European epic poetry, from Homer to Milton. Swift supervised their publication in Dublin and supplied a short account of the author. We have seen that Voltaire printed an edition of *La Henriade* in London in 1739. He had advertised for subscriptions in 1737 and George I, in the last year of his reign, headed the list of subscribers, besides awarding the author a gold medal and a sum of money equivalent to £250. When the edition appeared, it was dedicated to Queen Caroline, the wife of George II.

There were many more English than French subscribers, but this was partly due to the fact that most of the copies sent by Voltaire to Thieriot for distribution in France were lost or, it has been said, purloined by Thieriot.

---

[1] Lytton Strachey, ibid.

Voltaire also found time to write a first draft of his history of
Charles XII of Sweden and to work on his tragedy *Brutus*, not the
Brutus who figures in his tragedy of *La Mort de César*, which he
composed a few years later, but Brutus, the Roman consul in the
6th century BC, who defended Rome against Tarquin and condemned his own son to death. Voltaire had some difficulty in getting
Brutus accepted, partly because it upheld democratic government,
but the Comédie-Française staged it in 1730 with immediate success.
More surprisingly, when the history of Charles XII was printed
in Rouen it was seized by the police. Voltaire had no difficulty
in getting it reprinted and smuggled into Paris. It quickly acquired
popularity.

Altogether Voltaire spent nearly three years in England. We shall
see in the next chapter how strong and lasting an influence his
experiences there had upon his thoughts.

When Voltaire was permitted to return to France in March 1729,
he lodged with a wigmaker in the town of Saint-Germain-en-Laye,
just outside Paris. He was not given leave to reside in Paris itself
until the following month. The price which Louis XV made him
pay for this was the forfeiture of his pension, but Voltaire had more
than recouped himself by a manipulation of the State lottery which
netted him five hundred thousand francs. He renewed his friendship
with the Duc de Richelieu but this did not prevent him from charging interest on the money which Richelieu borrowed from him.

Voltaire's feelings of friendship were more severely tested in
March 1730, when Adrienne Lecouvreur died in his arms. Because
she had been an actress, her body was refused burial in consecrated
ground. This infuriated Voltaire who circulated a poem in protest.
As a result, he had to take refuge with his printer Claude-François
Jore who found a hiding-place for him in the neighbourhood of
Rouen. Later, when they had quarrelled over money, Jore complained that Voltaire had been niggardly in paying for his provisions
and in contributing to the wages of the servants whom Jore found
for him.

In 1731 Voltaire felt it safe to return to Paris. He found asylum
in the house, in the Palais Royal, of the Comtesse de Fontaine-

13

Martel, an elderly lady who kept a free-thinking salon of which he was the principal ornament. He put on a tragedy called *Eriphyle* which was only fairly well received. When his corrections of it failed to please those to whom he committed them, he abandoned it in favour of *Zaire*, a tragedy of which I shall give an account in the next chapter. We shall see that it is vaguely derivative of Shakespeare's *Othello*, though the resemblance, both in form and content, ends by being very slight. *Zaire* was performed at the Comédie-Française in August 1732. This was followed by a private performance in Madame de Martel's house, in which Voltaire, outrageously over-acting, took one of the leading parts, and by a performance at Court, arranged by the Duc de Richelieu.

Besides perfecting *Zaire*, Voltaire worked in this year on his *Lettres philosophiques*, alternatively entitled *Letters Concerning the English Nation*, the fruit of his experiences in England, which we shall later be examining in detail. He also found time to compose and publish a poem called *Le Temple du Goût*, in which he set out his canons of literary taste, and criticized various authors, including the unfortunate Jean-Baptiste Rousseau.

Madame de Martel died in 1733 and Voltaire had to find somewhere else to live. He took lodgings in a humble alley opposite the church of Saint-Gervais. The reason for his choice was that it made him a neighbour of Monsieur Demoulin, a grain and straw merchant who had devised a method of making paper out of straw. Voltaire supplied the capital for this venture, from which he made a satisfactory profit.

One evening three persons of fashion came to these lodgings to call on Voltaire. One of them was the Marquise du Châtelet, with whom Voltaire immediately started a love affair which lasted for sixteen years until her death. Émilie du Châtelet was the daughter of the Baron de Breteuil who had already befriended Voltaire. She was born in December 1706 and married the Marquis du Châtelet-Lomont in her nineteenth year. Having borne him a daughter and a son, she felt free to take lovers. Madame du Deffand has left a very unfavourable account of her appearance, accusing her among other things of having fat arms and legs, enormous feet and a very small head with a pointed nose and a shapeless mouth containing few teeth and those decayed, but this unkind description is not borne out by Nattier's portrait of her, which depicts her not indeed as a beauty but as having a pleasant, forthcoming face. The portrait also bears out the verdict of more friendly observers that she had attractive green eyes. There appears to have been a better warrant for the charge which Madame du Deffand also brought against her of trying to embellish herself with 'curls, jew-jaws, precious stones, glass-ware, everything in profusion'.[1] Voltaire himself criticized her taste in dress. He is likely, in any case, to have been captivated less by her looks than by her personality and intelligence. Even Madame du Deffand credited her with 'a fairly good mind' while complaining that 'she preferred the study of the most abstract sciences to more agreeable knowledge'.[2] In fact Madame du Châtelet had a passion for geometry, in which she took lessons from Pierre Maupertuis, subsequently Voltaire's enemy, as we shall see, but then on good terms with him through their common admiration for Isaac Newton.

His being in love encouraged Voltaire in 1734 to stage another play, *Adélaïde du Guesclin*, to write the librettos for two operas for at least one of which, *Samson*, Rameau composed the music, and to begin work on his tragedy of *Alzire*, a melodrama set in Paris, which was successfully presented at the Comédie-Française in 1736 and remained a favourite among his poetic plays.

The *Lettres philosophiques* appeared in its English translation in London in 1733, without attracting very much attention. When in the following year the original text was printed by Jore in Rouen, and something very like it under Thieriot's supervision in Basle and many copies also found their way to Paris thanks to its being liberally pirated in Amsterdam, there was an outcry. The French did not have to wait for the appearance of Chauvin to be chauvinistic, and the authorities took offence at the implication that English institutions were superior to their own. A copy of the book was ceremo-

[1] See Theodore Besterman, op. cit., p. 180.
[2] Ibid., pp. 180-1.

niously burned and a warrant issued for Voltaire's arrest. Voltaire fled first to Holland and then to Cirey in Lorraine, where the Châtelets owned a château. Voltaire at once set about remodelling it to make it fit for his own accommodation.

Owing to the good offices of his friend d'Argental, the charge against Voltaire was soon suspended and he was allowed to return to Paris. He had, however, to flee again in 1736 when a poem of his, *Le Mondain*, thought to be impious, was found among the effects of the Bishop of Lucan and circulated in Paris without his knowledge. He was invited to Berlin by the Crown Prince Frederick, this being the first contact between them, but preferred again to seek safety in Holland. Before long he was back at Cirey with his Émilie. He had his own set of apartments, which communicated with hers by a secret staircase. Monsieur du Châtelet was frequently away serving with the army but raised no objection to the arrangements when he was at home. Voltaire and Émilie had a strict regime of work to which the fairly numerous visitors to the house were obliged to adapt themselves. They met chiefly at meals except when Voltaire, not always truly, proclaimed himself to be suffering from colic. Émilie had added the study of physics to that of geometry and Voltaire was chiefly engaged in multiplying the cantos of his epic poem *La Pucelle*, on the theme of Joan of Arc, a work then thought to be scandalous but more wearisome to the present reader. Ostensibly to fill the gaps in Émilie's knowledge of history, he also began work on two historical pieces, *Le Siècle de Louis XIV*, and the monumental *Essai sur les mœurs*, in which he sought to encompass the history of the world up to the eighteenth century. I shall be examining these works in a later chapter. There was a small theatre in the house at Cirey in which tragedies were staged, chiefly Voltaire's own, with their author frequently taking part, and operas in which Émilie sang. In 1738, they both competed, without each other's knowledge, for a prize offered by the Academy of Sciences for an essay on 'The Propagation of Fire', but neither was successful.

The harmony of Voltaire's existence at Cirey was slightly marred by a squabble with Jore over money and the pirating of Voltaire's works, and by a running quarrel with a shady character, the Abbé

Desfontaines. Voltaire had befriended the Abbé in 1725, by extricating him from prison where he had been sent on suspicion of sodomy, at that time a capital offence, but Desfontaines had turned against him, spread scandal about his life in England and made a series of attacks on him in print, culminating in a scurrilous pamphlet *La Voltairomanie* in the composition of which he was assisted by Jean-Baptiste Rousseau. Voltaire made a number of counter-attacks, including an 'Ode sur l'Ingratitude'. When d'Argental reproached Desfontaines for his perfidy, the Abbé said, 'One must live'. 'I don't see the necessity,' said d'Argental. It is for this alone that Desfontaines is worth remembering.

Voltaire's sister had died in 1726 and her daughters were orphaned when their father Monsieur Mignot died in 1727. Voltaire undertook to find husbands for them. The older, Marie-Louise, declined the husband whom Voltaire had picked out for her because she had fallen in love with a notary called Nicolas Charles Denis, whom she married with her uncle's approval early in 1738. She was then in her twenty-sixth year. Later in the same year Marie-Elisabeth made a more brilliant marriage with Nicolas-Joseph de Dompierre, lord of Fontaine d'Hornoy, treasurer-in-chief at Amiens. When she was widowed in 1756 she pleased her uncle even more by marrying the Marquis de Florian. Voltaire furnished both girls with handsome dowries.

The Crown Prince of Prussia became King Frederick II in 1740, at the age of 28. He is better known to history as Frederick the Great. The correspondence with Voltaire, which he had initiated in 1736, had continued with a great show of warmth on both sides. Frederick regarded Voltaire as his master in the art of writing French verse, to which he was himself addicted. Voltaire was always susceptible to flattery, especially when it came from royalty, and he was disposed to honour Frederick as a benevolent despot. The fact that no sooner had Frederick ascended the throne than he embarked on the war of the Austrian Succession did not trouble him. Or rather, he took advantage of it to find favour with the French Court, suggesting to the Minister, the aged Cardinal de Fleury, that he could help to make Frederick an ally of France. Frederick had no intention of letting Voltaire influence his foreign policy and, having induced Voltaire to visit him in Prussia in the winter of 1740, he was annoyed at having to pay his travelling expenses. Nevertheless he continued to admire Voltaire's poetry and sought to attach him to his own court.

Neither his dabbling in politics, nor his embarking on the career of a money-lender, which he did at this time, put anything of a brake on Voltaire's writing. His tragedy of *Mahomet* was first performed at Lille, where his elder niece Madame Denis was living with her husband, and after some difficulty, owing to the French court's suspicion of Voltaire's dealings with Frederick, a suspicion which Frederick surreptitiously fostered, it achieved performance at the Comédie-Française in August 1742. The first night was a triumph but the tragedy was withdrawn after three performances because it was believed that in attacking Mahomet, Voltaire was covertly attacking Christ. Nothing daunted, Voltaire dedicated the work to the Pope, Benedict XIV, who accepted the dedication. In the following year Voltaire staged the tragedy of *Mérope*, again an attack on tyranny, but this time tyranny of a secular rather than a religious type. It was an enormous success, earning for Voltaire more royalties than he received from any other of his plays. He hoped that its success would secure him election to the Académie Française, the society of forty 'immortals', which Cardinal Richelieu had founded in 1635, but he was disappointed. He failed also to secure admission to the French Academy of Sciences but obtained the greater honour, for a foreigner, of election to the English Royal Society.

In 1743 Voltaire again accepted an invitation from Frederick to visit Prussia. To the dismay of Madame du Châtelet, who still cared very much for Voltaire's company, though they had ceased to be lovers physically, he remained there for several weeks, first in Berlin and then in Bayreuth, where he paid court to Frederick's sister Ulricka, the future Queen of Sweden, and enjoyed the favours of the French Ambassador's cook. Voltaire explained to Frederick that he had satisfied himself with the cook because he did not have an army of three thousand men to carry off the princess.

The visit ended badly because, not for the first time or the last, each man tried unsuccessfully to trick the other. Voltaire was, and was believed by Frederick to be, an agent of the French. To disarm suspicion he wrote a letter to Frederick in which he made fun of the Bishop of Mirepoix, a member of the French government. Frederick sent the letter to the Bishop, and the Bishop informed Voltaire. Furious with Frederick, Voltaire returned to Cirey. By now Frederick had no illusions about Voltaire's character, but he continued to send him his French compositions for correction, and to plead for a sight of at least some cantos of *La Pucelle*.

For some time Voltaire had been writing affectionately to his elder niece, Madame Denis, and from his letters – tracked down, translated and published by the indefatigable Mr Besterman – it seems clear that they became lovers at least very soon after her husband's death in 1744. Madame Denis was fat and florid, but one can infer from his letters that this contributed to her attractions for Voltaire. A large proportion of the letters are in Italian, perhaps as a measure of prudence. It is probable that they wished to guard their secret from Madame du Châtelet, if not from the world at large. Sexual relations between uncle and niece were not then regarded, even by the Roman Catholic Church, as impermissibly incestuous.

Voltaire's brother Armand died in 1745, unreconciled to Voltaire, naming his younger niece's husband as his executor and bequeathing him the greater part of his fortune. He could not, however, avoid enriching Voltaire who was the residuary legatee of half the estate which Armand had inherited from their father.

Having quarrelled with Frederick, Voltaire renewed his efforts to ingratiate himself with the French Court. As part of an entertainment to celebrate the marriage of the Dauphin to Maria-Theresa of Spain he wrote a comedy, *La Princesse de Navarre*, for which Rameau wrote the music. For this he was given the post of Royal Historiographer and a pension. He wrote a poem, *Le Temple de la Gloire*, to celebrate the French victory over the English at the battle of Fontenoy. He collaborated again with Rameau on another court entertainment, *La Fête de Ramire*, to which he allowed Jean-

Jacques Rousseau to put the finishing touches. This was the first contact between them. Rousseau wrote Voltaire an obsequious letter, to which Voltaire returned a friendly reply.

The result of all this was that when the death of Président Bouhier left a seat vacant at the Académie Française, the King let it be known that it would not displease him if Voltaire were elected to fill it. This duly came about in May 1746. Voltaire was not entirely happy at owing this honour to his court entertainments rather than his tragedies, but at his induction into the Académie he delivered an elaborate oration in praise of French culture and its ornaments, including the King, the Duc de Richelieu, Montesquieu, Fontenelle, Voltaire's old enemy the playwright Crébillon and his old tutor L'Abbé d'Olivet.

It was not long before Voltaire blotted his copy-book at court by warning Madame du Châtelet in English that she was playing with knaves when she had lost a great deal of money at the Queen's card-table. The two of them fled to the Duchesse de Maine's country house at Sceaux, between Paris and Versailles, where Voltaire busied himself with his tragedy *Sémiramis*, which was moderately well received when the Comédie-Française produced it in 1748, and wrote five of his short stories, *Cosi-Sancta*, *Babouc*, *Zadig*, *Scarmentado* and *Micromégas*. Madame du Châtelet contrived to have them forgiven at court and Voltaire obtained the goodwill of the King's favourite, Madame de Pompadour.

In 1748 Voltaire and Madame du Châtelet travelled from Fontainebleau to Lunéville, where King Stanislas of Lorraine held his court, not far from Cirey. There she met the Marquis de Saint-Lambert, a captain in the army, ten years younger than herself, and fell violently in love with him. Voltaire made a scene when he surprised them together, but soon got over his jealousy, and wrote a charming epistle to Saint-Lambert. All would have been well had not Émilie found herself pregnant. Believing that her husband would view her saddling him with a bastard as an offence to his honour, she lured him back into her bed after an interval, it is believed, of eighteen years. She duly gave birth to a daughter but died shortly after, at the age of 42. There is no doubt that

Voltaire was deeply distressed by her loss.

For one thing, he had to find somewhere else to live. For the time being he lodged with Madame Denis in Paris in the rue Traversière where they staged plays in the attic, notably Voltaire's *Rome sauvée*, to which the Comédie-Française had preferred Crébillon's play on the same subject. It was a great success, which was repeated when Voltaire persuaded the Duchesse de Maine to let it be performed at her house. Voltaire had discovered a talented young actor called Le Kain to whom he lent money of which Le Kain was in need, predicting, correctly, that Le Kain would soon make his way to the top of his profession.

Meanwhile Frederick was continually pressing Voltaire to settle at his court. Voltaire was tempted to accept but wanted to bring Madame Denis with him. Frederick was opposed to this, just as he had refused to allow Madame du Châtelet to accompany Voltaire on his earlier visits. Finally they compromised by Frederick's undertaking to pay for Madame Denis's upkeep while Voltaire was away, besides paying for Voltaire's travelling expenses. Voltaire asked Louis XV for permission to leave France, half-hoping that it would be refused, but Louis was happy to let him go, depriving him only of his post of royal historiographer but allowing him to keep his pension.

Voltaire arrived in Berlin in July 1750. He was immediately made a Court Chamberlain, awarded the Order of Merit, and given rooms in the royal palaces both at Berlin and Potsdam. Though he was granted yet another pension, he was still on the look-out for opportunities to increase his fortune and he entered into a shady transaction with a local broker, called Abraham Hirschel, to make a profit out of dealing in Silesian bonds. The two men fell out. There was a law-suit which Voltaire won, but his reputation suffered. Even before his arrival in Berlin he had annoyed Frederick by making fun of Frederick's letters to him and Frederick had referred to him as a malicious monkey. Nevertheless he was a highly talented monkey, as he showed, if more proof were required, by the publication in Berlin in 1752 of his historical work *Le Siècle de Louis XIV*, and Frederick needed him to add lustre to his court.

He needed him all the more as the intellectual cronies whom he had succeeded in assembling were, with one exception, nothing to boast of. As Lytton Strachey put it in his spirited essay 'Voltaire and Frederick', reprinted in his *Books and Characters*:

> There was hardly one of them that was not thoroughly second-rate. Algarotti was an elegant dabbler in scientific matters – he had written a book to explain Newton to the ladies; d'Argens was an amiable and erudite writer of a dull free-thinking turn; Chasot was a retired military man with too many debts, and Darget was a good-natured secretary with too many love affairs; La Mettrie was a doctor who had been exiled from France for atheism and bad manners; and Pöllnitz was a decaying baron who, under stress of circumstances, had unfortunately been obliged to change his religion six times.

The one exception was Pierre Louis Moreau de Maupertuis, Madame du Châtelet's tutor in geometry, whose fame as a geometer had secured him election to the French Academy of Sciences in 1723 at the early age of 25. The first Frenchman to become a member of the English Royal Society, he was also senior to Voltaire in the Académie Française, having obtained the chair left vacant by the death of Cardinal de Fleury in 1743, and had accepted Frederick's invitation to become President of the Prussian Royal Academy of Science and Letters in 1746. A man of imperious temper, he saw Voltaire's arrival in Berlin as a threat to his intellectual pre-eminence. For his part, Voltaire was not disposed to play second fiddle. Though they were once on good terms, it was predictable that they would quarrel.

The quarrel, when it came, was precipitated by Maupertuis' high-handedness. He was a physicist as well as a geometer and was especially proud of his discovery of the so-called Principle of Least Action, according to which, in its most general form, whenever there is a change in Nature, the quantity of action necessary for this change is the least possible. In 1751 a Swiss mathematician called Samuel Koenig, a professor of jurisprudence at The Hague and librarian to the Prince of Orange, published a memoir in Leipzig in which he objected to some of the consequences that Maupertuis had derived from this law and remarked that to the extent that they were true they had been anticipated in a letter written by Leibniz. He did not possess a copy of the letter but remembered having read it. Koenig, another of Madame du Châtelet's instructors in geometry, was a protégé of Maupertuis, who had been responsible for making him a corresponding member of the French Academy of Sciences in 1740 and a foreign member of the Berlin Academy in 1749. Before publishing his memoir, Koenig visited Berlin to discuss the question with Maupertuis, and even offered not to pursue the argument in print, but Maupertuis offended him by losing his temper. When Koenig's memoir appeared, Maupertuis, with the support of the mathematician Euler, its most distinguished member, called a meeting of his Academy for the purpose of declaring the letter attributed to Leibniz a fraud and Koenig a forger. Koenig responded in a dignified fashion and resigned his foreign membership.

This gave Voltaire his opportunity. Having prudently withdrawn his money from Berlin, he published an article entitled 'Réponse d'un Académicien de Berlin à un Académicien de Paris', which was a crushing statement of Koenig's case against Maupertuis. Frederick was infuriated and himself published a pamphlet, denouncing the author of the article as a worthless libeller. There the matter rested for a time until Maupertuis rashly brought out a volume of letters in which he dabbled in metaphysics. Voltaire's response was the famous satirical *Diatribe du docteur Akakia*, of which I shall later be giving an account. Frederick, when shown the manuscript, was highly amused but made Voltaire promise not to publish it. Very soon thousands of copies were circulating in Holland, Paris and throughout Germany. Frederick had copies publicly burned in Berlin. Voltaire returned his pension, his Order and the golden key which was his badge of office as Court Chamberlain. Surprisingly, Frederick insisted on his keeping them and persuaded Voltaire to remain for another three months, continuing to grace Frederick's table at supper at Potsdam, in the absence of Maupertuis who had taken to his bed. But by now Voltaire had had enough and on 26 March 1753 he left Berlin, taking with him a privately printed copy of Frederick's poems.

By the end of April Voltaire had reached Frankfurt where he was soon to be joined by Madame Denis. By this time Frederick had remembered about his poems and was frightened of the use to which Voltaire might put them. He had no jurisdiction over Frankfurt but his agent Baron Franz von Freytag was powerful enough to have Voltaire detained. The poems were recovered but it was over two months before Voltaire, Madame Denis and Voltaire's secretary, Collini, were able to leave Frankfurt. Voltaire gives an amusing account of the affair in his Memoirs which were posthumously published, though written in 1759. He and Frederick never met again and for a time there was a coolness between them; but twenty years later Frederick was again sending his French verses to Voltaire for correction, and Voltaire was paying him compliments in return.

After leaving Frankfurt Voltaire searched for another place to live. He had not yet received permission to return to Paris. He spent some time at Colmar and at Plombières and even stayed with Benedictine monks at their abbey of Sénones. He enjoyed their company but also took advantage of their excellent library to discover anti-religious material for the *Encyclopédie*, of which the first volume had been published in 1751, under the editorship of Denis Diderot and Jean d'Alembert. Voltaire had met d'Alembert in 1746 and immediately made friends with him. In a later chapter we shall be examining Voltaire's involvement with the *Encyclopédistes*.

In the winter of 1754–5 Voltaire decided to settle in Switzerland. He bought a town house at Montriond on the outskirts of Lausanne and soon afterwards paid a large sum for an estate which he christened 'Les Délices', at Saint-Jean near Geneva. In theory, Catholics were forbidden to own property in the territory of Calvinist Geneva, but thanks to his friendship with Doctor Theodore Tronchin and Tronchin's powerful family, Voltaire was exempted from the rule.

Voltaire spared no expense in embellishing Les Délices and this of course included supplying it with a theatre. Le Kain and France's leading actress, Mademoiselle Clairon, enjoyed a success there both in a revival of *Zaire* and in Voltaire's latest tragedy, *L'Orphelin de la Chine*, which was also performed before the court at Fontaine-bleau. When the Calvinist Consistory of Geneva forbade theatrical performances in its territory, Voltaire staged them at Montriond.

The occurrence of the Lisbon Earthquake in 1755 created a problem for the defenders of the Christian faith, since it called into question either God's omnipotence or his benevolence. Voltaire was quick to make this point in his *Poème sur la désastre de Lisbonne*. A Genevese pastor asked Jean-Jacques Rousseau to come to the aid of Providence and Rousseau obliged with a letter in which he sharply criticized Voltaire. It may have annoyed him that Voltaire declined to be drawn into controversy, even going so far as to commend the style of the letter. A few months earlier Voltaire had written very warmly to Rousseau in praise of his *Discours sur l'inégalité*, eliciting a grateful reply.

The outbreak of the Seven Years War was distressing to Voltaire because of his ambivalence towards Frederick who became the enemy of France through France's alliance with Austria. At various times he made ineffective attempts to induce the French Minister the Duc de Choiseul to negotiate for peace. He was however gratified at the outset by his friend the Duc de Richelieu's victory at Port Mahon over an English force commanded by Admiral Byng. When Admiral Byng was court-martialled for his failure, both Voltaire and Richelieu pleaded on his behalf. Notoriously, they failed to save him and he was shot on his own quarter-deck. This produced one of Voltaire's most famous sayings: 'In this country it is thought well to kill an admiral from time to time to encourage the others.'[1]

In the same year, 1756, Voltaire parted with Collini, mainly because of the mutual dislike between Collini and Madame Denis. Collini was replaced as secretary by Jean-Louis Wagnière who served Voltaire faithfully for the long remainder of Voltaire's life.

The puritanism of its clergy made the neighbourhood of Geneva dangerous for Voltaire. It became even more so in December 1757 with the publication in the *Encyclopédie* of d'Alembert's critical essay on Geneva, which Voltaire was known to have inspired. Conse-

[1]*Candide*, Ch. 23.

quently, without relinquishing Les Délices, he sought a refuge else-where and found it at Ferney, a small estate in Lorraine. Shortly afterwards he acquired a life-interest in the neighbouring estate of Tournay, the possession of which carried with it the title of Count. Voltaire rented Tournay from a Burgundian magistrate, Le Président de Brosses. The Président was not only a lawyer but an author who had published works on geography, linguistics and one entitled *Culte des dieux fétiches*, on the origin of the religions of Egypt. For a time the two men treated each other with mutual respect, but two or three years later had a ridiculous quarrel over fourteen loads of wood, supplied to Voltaire by a neighbouring peasant, Charles Baudry, and costing 281 francs which Voltaire refused to pay, claiming that the wood was a present to him from de Brosses. In the acrimonious correspondence which followed, de Brosses had no difficulty in showing that this claim was false and having gained a moral victory, the Président brought the business to an end by settling with Baudry and persuading Voltaire to contribute 281 francs to charity. Ten years later, Voltaire had his revenge by pre-venting the Fetish, as he then called him, from being elected to the seat in the Académie Française which his writings had earned him. Lytton Strachey gives a most amusing account of this whole affair in his 'The Président de Brosses', reprinted in his *Portraits in Miniature*.

The business of modelling his new estates to his satisfaction did not interfere with Voltaire's programme of literary work. In March 1759 he published in Geneva the book which has stood the test of time better than all the rest of his voluminous writings, the fable of *Candide*. As we shall see, it is a devastating satire directed against a literal acceptance of Leibniz's proposition that no possible world could be better than the actual world that God has created. In his *Confessions* Jean-Jacques Rousseau claimed never to have read *Candide*, but this is hard to believe. I suspect that it was at least partly responsible for the letter written to Voltaire in June 1760 in which Rousseau held Voltaire responsible for the corruption of Geneva, as well as his own difficulties with the authorities of his native city, and ended with a catalogue of his reasons for hating

Voltaire. Voltaire did not reply to this letter, though he wrote to Thieriot that Rousseau had gone mad. However, when Rousseau's *La Nouvelle Héloïse* came out in 1761, Voltaire attacked it in four letters, none of them written under his own name.

It was in 1759 that Voltaire first issued his famous battle-cry 'écrasez l'infâme'. The term 'l'infâme', signifying what needed to be crushed, appears to have been suggested to Voltaire by Frederick, who had already resumed their correspondence. Voltaire used it to comprehend not only the evils resulting from religious bigotry and superstition but also the abuse of power in any form. We shall be seeing how disgraceful a part religion played in the Calas case, which occupied Voltaire from 1761 to 1763, as it did in the case of Sirven, which dragged on from 1760 to 1765, and that of the Chevalier de la Barre in 1766, perhaps the most atrocious of all; but Voltaire also exerted himself to obtain the posthumous rehabilitation of the Comte de Lally-Tollendal, who had been wrongfully condemned and executed for treason, to save the life of Madame Montbailli, whose husband had been tortured to death on a charge of murder which it was obvious that they had not committed, to achieve the liberation of a colony of serfs at Saint-Claude in the Jura, not only because their oppressors were a community of monks, and to right other injustices besides. In 1763 he published his *Traité sur la tolérance*.

It illustrates the complexity of Voltaire's character that while he was totally serious in his policy of combating 'l'infâme', he could easily blind himself to the excesses of those whom he chose to extol as benevolent despots. We shall see that he regarded the century of Louis XIV as a golden age and that in his *Histoire de l'empire de Russie sous Pierre le Grand*, which occupied him from 1751 to 1763, he plays down Peter's brutality in favour of his civilizing influence. His quarrel with Frederick was personal; we have seen that he was ready to be cajoled by him so long as they kept their mutual distance; he never really saw Frederick as the ruthless warmonger that he primarily was. The most striking example is to be found in his relations with the Empress of Russia, Catherine the Great. She initiated a correspondence which lasted from 1762 to 1777, the year before his death. The tone of their letters is consistently that of mutual flattery. He makes light of her murder of her husband. He almost applauds her share in the partition of Poland. He enthusiastically supports her in her war against Mustapha III, the Sultan of Turkey, as if her motive for trying to annex Constantinople were to achieve the liberation of Greece. He saw her only in the light of her professions of support for the *philosophes*. She bought Diderot's library. She had herself inoculated against smallpox at a time when inoculation was forbidden in France. She did not engage in religious persecution. What if she did omit to free the Russian serfs? For her part Catherine was unstinting in her expressions of admiration for Voltaire's genius; she instructed her courtiers, diplomats and men of letters to visit him at Ferney; but she took care not to invite him to Russia in return.

The name of Jean-Jacques Rousseau is often associated with that of Voltaire in the campaign against 'l'infâme'. For instance, when Boswell asked Dr Johnson in 1766 whether he thought Rousseau as bad a man as Voltaire, Johnson said, 'Why, Sir, it is difficult to settle the proportion of iniquity between them.' In fact, as we have already noted, they were by no means consistently allied. It is true that Voltaire's *Le Sermon des cinquante*, a repudiation of the scriptures, was followed by a work in the same spirit, Rousseau's more celebrated *La Profession de foi du vicaire savoyard*, but when Voltaire proceeded, while disclaiming its authorship, to publish *Saul*, a violent attack on the Old Testament, Rousseau denounced not only *Saul* but Voltaire as its author. This so enraged Voltaire who had already been provoked, in 1764, by Rousseau's accusing him in his *Lettres de la montagne* of being responsible for his banishment from Geneva that in a pamphlet called *Le Sentiment des citoyens* he actually took the side of the Genevese pastors against Rousseau, whom he described truly as a vagabond, untruly as an unsuccessful writer and a debauchee, but truly again as one who had abandoned all his children to orphanages. After that, Voltaire was mainly content to ridicule Rousseau in his correspondence with others, though he again attacked him publicly in 1768 in a satirical poem *La Guerre civile de Genève* in which he made fun, among other things, of the

Genevese council's intolerance of fornication.

Boswell's visit to Voltaire took place in 1764, when Boswell was 24. The letter to Madame Denis in which he successfully angled for an invitation to supper and to stay the night is characteristically ingenuous, but although in the course of recommending himself to Jean-Jacques Rousseau he naïvely described Voltaire's conversation as the most brilliant that he had ever heard, his summary of it amounts to little more than a testimony to Voltaire's hatred of religion, coupled with his belief in the existence of a Supreme Being. Gibbon, who called on Voltaire in the previous year, was more fortunate in that he witnessed a performance of *L' Orphelin de la Chine* with Voltaire and Madame Denis in the leading parts, and afterwards stayed to supper. His impressions of the occasion are recorded in a letter to his step-mother. I quote them in part:

> Perhaps ... I was too much struck with the ridiculous figure of Voltaire at seventy acting a Tartar Conqueror with a hollow broken Voice, and making love to a very ugly niece of about fifty. The play began at eight in the evening and ended (entertainment and all) about half an hour after eleven. The whole Company was asked to stay and sat Down about twelve to a very elegant supper of a hundred Covers. The supper ended about two, the company danced till four; when we broke up, got into our Coaches and came back to Geneva just as the Gates were opened. Show me in history or fable, a famous poet of seventy who has acted in his own plays and has closed the scene with a supper and ball for a hundred people. I think the last is the more extraordinary of the two.

Voltaire's dress at this period is well described by the Prince de Ligne who also visited him at Ferney in 1763. 'He always wore grey slippers, iron-grey stockings, with the tops rolled down, a large cotton damask jacket down to the knees, a great long wig, and a little black velvet cap. Sometimes on Sundays he would put on a fine bronze-coloured suit with coat and breeches to match, but the coat had wide skirts, gold braid, scallops, and embroidery, with lace cuffs down to his finger tips; he said that such a costume made him look distinguished.' The implication is that Voltaire adhered to the fashion of his youth.

So many visitors came to Ferney that Voltaire announced in 1764 that he could no longer be relied upon to appear at dinner. There was also a large more or less permanent establishment. Besides Madame Denis and Wagnière this included by 1768 a Jesuit, Father Adam, with whom Voltaire played chess, a copyist Simon Bigex, a young writer Jean François de la Harpe and his wife, and Corneille's great niece, Marie, her husband Pierre-Jacques Dupuits and their children. Not only were there fifty or sixty servants on the estate, but a number of workers, who were employed in the manufacture of silk and lace and above all in the production of watches. Voltaire lured his watchmakers from Geneva, where they were in dispute with their employers, and took care that the watches that they made for him should be of the finest quality. He then exerted himself to promote their sale. He sent the first of them, like the first pair of silk stockings manufactured at Ferney, to Madame de Choiseul in Paris. He solicited orders from all his noble friends and acquaintances. The agency for Spain was forced upon the French Ambassador. Cardinal de Bernis in Rome was cajoled into accepting a case of watches for purchase by his fellow cardinals. A quantity went to Catherine the Great. Even the Sultan of Turkey was approached, but it is not known with what result.

While enriching himself in this way, Voltaire continued to lend money at interest to German princes and French noblemen, to place funds in banks and businesses in Cadiz and Leipzig and Amsterdam, and to take out life annuities which he obtained on good terms because of his age and what Collini called 'his cadaverous face'. He owed this appearance partly to the loss of his teeth, partly to his sparse diet, consisting, if his visitors are to be trusted, mainly of a series of cups of coffee, taken with a little cream, partly to the purgatives which he was constantly taking, partly perhaps to actual infirmities. If this last point is open to doubt, the reason is that in spite of his perpetual insistence, even before he reached the age of sixty, that he was on the brink of death, he lived to be eighty-three, without any marked loss of energy, or diminution of his literary production, or loss of his enthusiasm for cultivating his friends or harassing his enemies.

In 1764 Voltaire brought out his pocket dictionary of philosophy, with an enlarged edition published in the following year. We shall see that it is not, any more than his *Lettres philosophiques*, a work of philosophy, as the term is now understood, but a series of Voltaire's pithy reflections upon a set of topics, somewhat arbitrarily chosen and arranged in alphabetical order. He had been working intermittently on this *Dictionnaire philosophique* since he stayed at the court of Frederick the Great. It is so thoroughly in the spirit of 'écrasez l'infâme' and his wit appears in it to such advantage that next to *Candide* it remains the most popular of all Voltaire's writings.

We have seen that Voltaire's last overt attack on Jean-Jacques Rousseau occurred in 1768 as part of a poem in which he satirized Geneva. If only because the citizens of Geneva were the mainstay of the audience for his theatrical performances at Ferney, Voltaire had no wish to be put on a Genevese blacklist, and he showed the manuscript of *La Guerre civile de Genève* only to the members of his household and to privileged visitors. He was therefore horrified to discover that printed copies were circulating both in Geneva and Paris. After accusing at least one innocent person, he discovered that the culprit was La Harpe, abetted by Madame Denis. In a fury Voltaire banished them both from Ferney, together with all its other habitués except for the faithful Wagnière and Father Adam, whom Voltaire still needed for his games of chess. Voltaire did not care for it to be known that his niece's avarice had gone to the lengths of her robbing him, so he put it about that he had sent her to Paris to collect money that was owed to him. For her part Madame Denis preferred Paris to Ferney as a place to live, but she was frightened of jeopardizing her inheritance and therefore frequently asked to be allowed to return. Voltaire eventually acceded to her request and received her back with open arms. Their separation had lasted for eighteen months.

Voltaire had rebuilt the parish church at Ferney in 1761 and adorned it with the proud inscription in letters of gold *Deo erexit Voltaire* ('Built for God by Voltaire'). One Easter Sunday it struck

31

his fancy to take communion at this church and to preach a sermon on theft, there having been some pilfering on the estate of Ferney. Since he had no authority to preach he received a mild rebuke from the Bishop of Annecy, in whose diocese Ferney was included. Annoyed by the bishop, Voltaire staged an elaborate farce the following Easter. Feigning to be on the point of death, he forced the parish priest of Ferney, a genuinely sick man, and a visiting Capuchin prior to give him communion in his own bedroom and to absolve him from his sins. When the clergymen had gone he sprang out of bed, saying to Wagnière that it had been good fun and proposing a walk round the garden. This performance shocked both his Christian enemies and his free-thinking friends. It may have been in the course of it that when the fire in his bedroom burned up he remarked 'les flammes déjà!' (the flames already), if he ever said this at all. Contrary to popular belief, there is no good evidence that these were actually his dying words.

Nothing, neither his domestic concerns, nor his bickering with the church, nor the upkeep of his estate, nor his commercial transactions, nor his pursuit of justice, nor his vast correspondence, nor the procession of visitors to Ferney, could stem the flow of Voltaire's literary production. In the 1760s, as we shall see, he was chiefly occupied with works of history, finding time also for five more of his prose tales and about as many comedies in verse. Even so he did not foresake his first love of poetic drama. *Tancrède*, a drama of the age of chivalry, dedicated to Madame de Pompadour and venturing on romanticism, was staged to applause in Paris in the autumn of 1760, after a successful try-out in the tiny theatre at Tournay. It had been preceded in the same year by two of Voltaire's more mediocre works, the comedy *L'Écossaise* and tragedy, *La Mort de Socrate*. Taste was changing and *L'Olympie*, which was performed at Ferney in 1763 and in Paris the year after, was not so well received. Voltaire had better hopes of *Les Lois de Minos*, a denunciation of outmoded laws, which he sent to Catherine, but he fell foul of the censor when he tried to get it performed in Paris. He had to be content with publishing the text in 1773. Meanwhile *Les Scythes*, in which it has been conjectured that the Scythians were intended to portray the Genevese and that Voltaire projected himself into the character of a benevolent Persian general, was much applauded at Ferney but booed in Paris. It was followed by *Les Guèbres* (The Parsees) which resembled *L'Olympie* in that it took Voltaire only six days to write. Commenting on *L'Olympie*, d'Alembert expressed the hope that Voltaire would not imitate God by resting on the seventh day.

Somewhat surprisingly Father Adam was in the habit of celebrating mass at Ferney, with Voltaire's approval. The trouble was that Father Adam was bald and priests were not allowed to wear wigs when saying mass, with the result that Father Adam caught cold. Voltaire took advantage of the election of a new Pope, Clement XIV, in 1769 to write to his old friend Cardinal de Bernis in Rome asking him to obtain a dispensation from the new Pope for Father Adam to celebrate mass in his wig. The dispensation was granted. In theory, the consent of the Bishop of Annecy was also needed, but Voltaire and Father Adam did not wait upon a condition which they knew would not be satisfied.

Much as Voltaire enjoyed being monarch of all that he surveyed at Ferney, and a genuine benefactor of his people, he chafed at his exile from Paris. Neither the good relations which he was careful to maintain with Madame de Pompadour nor the influence of friends at court, like d'Argental, were sufficient to induce Louis XV to lift the ban. When Louis XV died in 1774 Voltaire hoped that the old king's grandson and successor Louis XVI would relent towards him. Louis XVI did nothing, but after taking careful soundings Voltaire decided that if he were to come to Paris, even without the king's express permission, no serious action would be taken against him.

The occasion which he chose for his return was the first performance at the Comédie-Française of his latest tragedy *Irène*, which he advertised as depicting the remorse of a woman who loved her husband's murderer. He left Ferney by coach on 3 February 1778, accompanied by Wagnière; Madame Denis had gone ahead. The coach reached Dijon on 7 February and Paris on 10 February. Voltaire, Wagnière; and Madame Denis all stayed at the house of the Marquis de Villette at the corner of the rue de Beaune and the quai du Theatins, now renamed the quai Voltaire. The Marquis de Villette, the son of a self-made man who had bought the title, had corresponded with Voltaire and found favour with him by coming to Ferney in 1777 and marrying Mademoiselle de Varicourt, a protégée of Voltaire's, without a dowry. Even so it seems curious that Voltaire should have put himself under his care in Paris rather than stay with one of his older friends. Perhaps the luxury of the Marquis' establishment appealed to Madame Denis.

No sooner was it known that Voltaire was in Paris than a stream of callers arrived at the house where he was staying. They were filtered by Madame Denis and Madame de Villette and received by Voltaire in his dressing-gown. D'Argental, who was one of the first to come, brought the bad news that Le Kain, whom Voltaire wanted for the leading part in *Irène*, had died on 8 February. The Académie Française held a formal meeting on 12 February and the fifteen members present unanimously resolved that an official deputation should wait upon Voltaire. The deputation was voted to consist of the Prince de Beauvau, M. de Marmontel and M. de Saint-Lambert, but most of the others, including d'Alembert, who as secretary had proposed the motion, came as well. The British Ambassador, Lord Stormont, called, as did the composer Gluck, and Benjamin Franklin bringing his fifteen-year-old grandson, whom Voltaire blessed, saying in English 'God and Liberty'. The blind Madame du Deffand called and reported that Voltaire was ill.

She was right. Being constantly on show at the age of eighty-three was too much even for Voltaire and within three weeks of his arrival he was spitting blood. He was not afraid of death as such, but remembering the fate of Adrienne Lecouvreur, he was horrified by the thought that his corpse would be dumped on a rubbish heap. He therefore chose to make his peace with the church. It happened that Father Gautier, a Jesuit not previously known to him, had written to offer him his services and Voltaire accepted them. On 2 March in Father Gautier's presence he wrote a recantation, the import of which was that he was dying in the Catholic faith into which he had been born, that he hoped for God's mercy and forgiveness of his sins, and that if he had ever offended the Church he asked for its pardon and for God's. Voltaire's nephew, the Abbé Mignot, and the Marquis de Vielleville were then called in as witnesses to Voltaire's signature. When they and Father Gautier had gone, Wagnière reproached Voltaire for his apostasy. Voltaire then wrote for Wagnière's benefit, 'I die, worshipping God, loving my friends, not hating my enemies and detesting superstition.' In any case, he had not taken communion, telling Father Gautier that he did not wish to mix his blood with God's. Later he exchanged courteous letters with M. de Tersac, the curé of Saint-Sulpice, before whom his recantation should officially have been made.

After this Voltaire's health improved. He was well enough by 30 March to attend the first performance of *Irène* at the Comédie-Française. The occasion was a triumph for him. On his way to the theatre he stopped at the Louvre which was then the meeting-place of the Académie Française. The Academicians presented filed before him and d'Alembert made a speech in his honour, coupling his name with those of Racine and Boileau. A large crowd gathered in the courtyard and accompanied him to the theatre, where the whole audience rose to greet him. When he was seated in his box between Madame Denis and Madame de Villette, the actor Brizac, who had taken the part destined for Le Kain, crowned him with a laurel wreath. At the end of the play a bust of Voltaire was brought on the stage and wreathed in flowers. The leading actress, Madame Vestris, came forward and read some verses the burden of which was that Voltaire was already immortal and that France had given him his crown. The subsequent performance of *Le Ninon*, one of Voltaire's slighter comedies, might have been an anti-climax, but the audience barely listened to it. It was too busy applauding Voltaire.

Though he was equal to this occasion, Voltaire was still in poor health; he could hardly ask for any greater honour to be paid to him in Paris and if he was going to recuperate he stood a better chance of doing so in Ferney. Both Wagnière and Dr Tronchin advised him to return to Ferney but the Villettes and Madame Denis pressed him to remain in Paris. In Madame Denis' case at least the motive was cupidity. She was terrified that her uncle would revoke the will that he had made largely in her favour two years before and she went so far as to intercept the letters which Voltaire wrote to his lawyer. It is understandable that Voltaire should have been tempted to prolong his stay in Paris, after an exile of twenty-eight years, but the decision was fatal to him. He found the energy to undergo the ceremony of initiation into the Freemason's lodge of the Nine-Sisters on 7 April and a month later to attend a meeting of the Académie, at which he persuaded them to undertake the production of an authoritative French dictionary, a task on which the Académie is working to this day. After that his health gave out completely. He was afflicted with cancer of the prostate and he suffered great pain. Dr Tronchin could do nothing for him and Wagnière who might at least have seen that he was properly nursed had been sent back to Ferney. The details of Voltaire's physical decline and neglect are squalid. He died on 30 May 1778, nearly six months short of his eighty-fourth birthday. Most probably, his last words were 'Laissez-moi en paix'.

What of his hope that his body would receive a Christian burial? It was fulfilled thanks to the ingenuity of his nephew, the Abbé Mignot. It was obvious that no such ceremony would be permitted in Paris but M. Mignot held a position of authority at the Benedictine monastery of Scellières in the neighbourhood of Troyes. Accordingly, early on 31 May he called in a surgeon and an apothecary who performed an autopsy on Voltaire's body and embalmed it, having removed the brain, which the apothecary M. Mithouart was allowed to keep, and the heart, which was secured by the Marquis de Villette. The mummy was then dressed, put on to a coach and driven out of Paris to Scellières. A second coach followed, containing Voltaire's great-nephew M. Dompierre d'Hornoy and two distant cousins. The Abbé Mignot had gone ahead, armed with the recantation which Voltaire had made before Father Gautier, to persuade the prior, Dom Protherat de Corbière, that everything was in order. The prior was satisfied and Voltaire's body was buried with due ceremony in the presence of four of his relatives. It had been placed in a wooden coffin. M. Mignot would have preferred the coffin to be of lead but Madame Denis had objected to the expense. When reproached by the Bishop of Troyes, the prior wrote an admirable letter in his own defence. An attempt was made to dismiss him by his superior the Abbot of Pontigny, but I am glad to say that it was unsuccessful.

It was customary when a member of the Académie died for a service to be held at the Church of the Cordeliers, belonging to the Franciscan friars. In Voltaire's case the friars refused to follow this precedent. D'Alembert was equally unsuccessful in his approach to other church authorities in Paris and the Bishop of Geneva in accord with the local Protestants, made sure that no service was held at Ferney. Finally d'Alembert had recourse to the Freemasons and an elaborate ceremony in Voltaire's honour was held at the Nine-Sisters lodge on 28 November. D'Alembert also persuaded the Académie to make Voltaire the subject of the poem for which it offered a gold medal in 1779 and to double the usual value of the award.

The task of bringing out a complete edition of Voltaire's works was undertaken at ruinous cost to himself by Pierre de Beaumarchais, celebrated as the author of *The Barber of Séville* and *The Marriage of Figaro*. It came out between 1782 and 1789 and ran to seventy-two volumes with an introduction and notes by Condorcet. It is known as the Kehl edition because of the place in which it was printed, and has been supplemented in our own time by Mr Theodore Besterman's collection of Voltaire's correspondence.

The value of Voltaire's estate has been estimated at a thousand million francs in present-day terms. He bequeathed a year's wages to his servants, a small legacy to Wagnière and more generous legacies to the Abbé Mignot and M. Dompierre d'Hornoy. Half the estate went to Madame Denis, who lost no time in selling Voltaire's library to Catherine the Great and Ferney to the Marquis de Villette, making a good bargain in each case. She then married a former dragoon called Duvivier, variously described as ten and thirty years younger than herself. Whatever their respective ages they quickly squandered Voltaire's fortune.

Voltaire's corpse remained at Scellières till 1791 when the coffin was brought in triumph to Paris and installed in the Panthéon. Homage was paid to it there until the 1860s when the coffin was opened and found to be empty. It was discovered that some fanatics had pillaged both Voltaire's and Rousseau's coffins as long before as 1814 and thrown the contents on a rubbish heap where they had disappeared without trace. The jar containing Voltaire's brain was put up for auction by an employee of the Mithouard family and went to an unknown buyer. Only Voltaire's heart is known to survive. It was bequeathed by the third Marquis de Villette to the Bishop of Orléans who had no thought but to sell it. Napoleon III acquired it and gave it to the National Library in Paris. It is there to this day together with the products of his brain.

2

The English Influence

Go into the London Exchange, a place of more dignity than many courts, you will find representatives of all nations assembled there to promote human welfare; there the Jew, the Mahometan and the Christian deal with one another as though they were of the same religion; the only persons whom they count as infidels are those who go bankrupt; there the Presbyterian trusts the Anabaptist and the Anglican accepts the Quaker's promise. When they leave these peaceful and free assemblies, some go to the Synagogue, others go to have a drink, this one goes to have himself baptized in a large cistern in the name of the Father proceeding via the Son to the Holy Ghost: that one has his son's foreskin cut off, mumbling over the child some Hebrew words which he does not understand: those others go to their Church with their hats on waiting for divine inspiration, and all are content.

If there were only one religion in English, there would be a risk of despotism, if there were two they would cut each other's throats; as it is, there are thirty, and they live happily in peace.

These are the concluding paragraphs of the sixth of the seven letters concerning the varieties of religious belief and practice in England, with which Voltaire begins his *Lettres philosophiques*. He does not substantiate his claim to have discovered so many as thirty sects, and clearly did not mean it to be taken literally, though if

39

he had bothered to list all the sub-divisions of the Nonconformists, he could well have managed to reach double figures. In emphasizing, indeed over-emphasizing, the multiplicity of English religions he was less concerned with the fact itself than with what he took to be its effect, the prevalence in England of religious tolerance. This is a dominant note in the overall theme of the *Lettres philosophiques*, that matters were ordered better in England than in France.

In this connection, an important letter is the fifth, in which Voltaire discourses on the Anglican religion. He begins by remarking that an Englishman, as a free man, chooses his own path to heaven, but then weakens this tribute by saying that if one wishes to obtain employment in England or Ireland one has to adhere to the Church of England, with the result that ninety-five per cent of the population do so. Voltaire appears not to have noticed that this is inconsistent with his commendation of England for its religious tolerance, but he may have let this pass in view of his opinion that adherence to the Church of England was not a serious religious commitment. For instance, he asserts that a great many Nonconformists have been converted to it purely in order to remove a barrier to their employment. Writing as he was in the early part of the eighteenth century, Voltaire was most probably right in assuming, as one would be today, that the Anglican church was not pernickity about the beliefs of those whom it admitted into its fold. On the other hand he may well have underrated the zeal, as well as the numbers, of Nonconformists who would have regarded even the show of Anglicanism on their part as apostasy. It is strange also that he failed to mention Roman Catholicism, beyond remarking that the English clergy had preserved many Catholic ceremonies, especially that of receiving tithes. Since he was acquainted with Pope, he must have known that there still were Catholics in England, but he may have thought them not worth mentioning in view of their comparative rarity and lack of political influence. Where he was seriously at fault was in bringing Ireland within the scope of his generalization. His frequentation of Dean Swift and slight knowledge of Bishop Berkeley may have convinced him that the plums in Ireland were reserved for Anglicans, but he should not have overlooked the fact that the majority of the population was sincerely Catholic and that its condition stained the English radiance of religious toleration. The Scots he correctly treated as a special case.

The great merit of the Church of England, in Voltaire's eyes, was that it was subordinate to the State. Its bishops, to the number of twenty-six, might sit in the House of Lords, but they were swamped by the secular peers. In theory, the Church was favoured by the Tories and distrusted by the Whigs. In practice, the Tories took no steps to emancipate the Church from parliamentary control and the Whigs saw no reason to curtail its power, beyond forbidding the Assembly of the Lower Clergy. However galling it might be, especially to the Higher Clergy, they had to admit that they owed their benefices to lay patronage and not to divine right.

Amusingly, it seemed to Voltaire that the Anglican clergy had better morals than the French. He put it down to the fact that all of them were educated at Oxford and Cambridge, away from the licentiousness of London and that it was only very late in life that they attained to high office in the Church, when all their passions were exhausted except that of avarice. Moreover, the fact that most clergymen were married, coupled with the bad manners which they acquired at the university and the small part that women played in English social life, meant that bishops had as a rule to put up with being monogamous. Clergymen sometimes frequented public houses, this not being considered improper, and if they got drunk there, they did so seriously and unobtrusively. What was lacking in England was the hybrid between an ecclesiastic and a layman, known in France as an Abbé, a dissolute sybarite, becoming a prelate through feminine intrigue. By comparison English parsons were reverend and mostly pedants. If Voltaire meant to imply that this was a point in England's favour, he was being hypocritical, since he did not care for pedants, especially if their pedantry took a religious turn, and we have seen that there were many Abbés whose company he enjoyed.

If the average English parson was as virtuous as Cato when compared with a French Abbé, then Catos were men of pleasure when compared with Scottish Presbyterians. Voltaire equated Presbyterianism with Calvinism in its pure Genevan form. The dominant religion in Scotland, it had acquired a foothold in England, sufficient to install the English Sunday, which outdid the Catholic Church in its severity. Work and play were both forbidden; there were no operas, comedies or concerts performed in London on a Sunday. Only the upper classes and people of standing ventured even to have a game of cards. For the rest of the nation there were just sermons, public houses, and the company of whores.

In spite of their puritanism, Voltaire came to admire the Quakers, to whom he devoted no less than the first four of his *Philosophical Letters*. He was instructed in their doctrine by Edward Higginson, a schoolmaster's assistant at Wandsworth, and taken to one of their meetings by a prosperous linen-draper called Andrew Pitt. While he teased them for engaging in the contortions to which they owed their name, and for the stubborn simplicity of their dress, and could not take seriously their claim to be possessed by the holy spirit, he paid tribute to their sincerity and was awed by their way of life. He was impressed by their disregard of social distinctions, their staunchness under persecution, and their overall humanity. He forewent his irony to eulogize both George Fox, the founder of the sect, and William Penn, its most powerful member, depicting the State of Pennsylvania as a more idyllic haven than it probably ever was.

In some ways, the most interesting of the letters in which Voltaire treats of the state of religion in England at the time of his visit is the seventh and last, of which the subject is said to be Socinians, Arians, or Anti-Trinitarians. In fact, these classes are not equivalent, since Socinians resemble Deists in rejecting the divinity of Christ, the trinity and the doctrine of original sin, and differ from them at most in holding that those who follow Christ's virtues will be granted salvation; whereas Arians merely deny that the Son is of one substance with the Father, whatever that may mean, and one can presumably qualify as an Anti-Trinitarian by downgrading the Holy Ghost. Voltaire did not claim to have discovered any Socinians, at least as they are properly defined, but he did assert that the Arian heresy was gaining ground in England and named Isaac Newton and Samuel Clarke as its most illustrious adherents. He believed that the heresy would regain the popularity which it enjoyed for three hundred years before suffering twelve hundred years of neglect, were it not that the age was one in which people were sated with religious disputes and sects. I think it worth quoting his conclusion:

> Is it not strange that Luther, Calvin, Zwingli, all unreadable writers, founded sects which split Europe apart, that Mahomet, an ignoramus, gave Asia and Africa a religion, and that Messrs Newton, Clarke, Locke, Leclerc, and so on, the greatest philosophers and the best authors of their time, have bare'y succeeded in gathering a tiny flock, which grows less every day.
>
> That shows how important it is to be born at the right time. If Cardinal de Retz were to reappear today, he would not rouse ten women in Paris.
>
> If Cromwell were to be born again, Cromwell, who had his king's head cut off and made himself Sovereign, would be a simple London merchant.

From religion Voltaire turned to politics and to commerce. In his letter on Parliament his chief objects were to decry religion and to show once again how much better these matters were ordered in England than in France. He remarked that members of Parliament in England liked to compare themselves with the Ancient Romans, but he could not see that they had anything in common, except perhaps a disposition to sell their votes. The Ancient Romans were superior in so far as their civil wars were not religious. What turned the balance in favour of England was that whereas the civil wars in Rome led to tyranny, the civil wars in England, for all their religious tincture, led to liberty. On the other hand, the civil wars in France in the sixteenth and seventeenth centuries not only had the demerit of being religious, but were nothing but manifestations of cruelty and folly.

Voltaire may have misunderstood the formula 'the King can do no wrong' as an expression of the monarch's subservience to the law in England rather than his immunity from it. Nevertheless he was right in thinking that the successful rebellion against Charles I and the glorious revolution of 1688, which deposed James II, placed an enduring limitation upon the monarch's powers. Voltaire accepted the description of the English government by a contemporary English writer as 'aristocratic–democratic–monarchic' and endorsed the view of another that 'The Constitution of our English government (the best in the world) is a most excellently mixt or qualified Monarchy where the King is vested with large Prerogatives to support Majesty, and restrained only from the power of doing himself and People harm.' So impressed was Voltaire with the English form of government that he even idealized the foreign policy of Queen Anne's ministers, representing the war waged against Louis XIV as an attempt to endow Europe with the benefits of liberty.

The ensuing letter on the English government is largely historical. True to his dislike of the clergy of any sort as an organized body, Voltaire attributed to the Druids the same maleficence as to the Catholic prelates after the Norman conquest. He was particularly scornful of John Lackland for ceding his kingdom to the Pope. This was the King John who was forced to sign Magna Carta, but Voltaire shared his friend Bolingbroke's view that if the condition of the people, in point of liberty, thereafter very much improved, it was the accidental effect of the contests between the kings, the barons and the clergy. On Voltaire's reading of English history, Henry VII was the first king whose policy it was to strengthen the House of Commons at the expense of the House of Lords. When it came to his own time, Voltaire considered it a further mark of England's superiority to France that taxes were proportionate to property and that it was the House of Commons and not the House of Lords, with its bishops, that had the powers of initiating measures of finance.

'By trade and commerce,' wrote Bolingbroke, 'we grew a rich and powerful nation.' Voltaire echoed this judgement in his letter on Commerce. If England, a small island with comparatively few natural resources, had become a great power it was owing to the strength of its navy, and the navy had been developed to safeguard

English trade. By spreading wealth, trade promotes liberty and liberty in its turn spreads trade. Once again the letter concludes with a paragraph which is invidious to the French:

> In France anyone who chooses is a Marquis and anyone who comes to Paris from the depths of the provinces with money to spend and a name ending in *ac* or *ille* can speak of 'a man like me, a man of my quality' and display a sovereign contempt for men of business; and the businessman hears so much contemptuous talk of his profession that he is fool enough to be ashamed of it; all the same I don't know who does the greater service to the State, a powdered Lord who knows exactly when the King gets up and when he goes to bed, and gives himself airs in playing the part of a slave in a minister's waiting-room, or a businessman who enriches his country, gives orders from his office to Surat and to Cairo, and adds to the sum of human happiness.

Here Voltaire, in his campaign against the French, may have been too indulgent to the English. It is, however, possible that the disdain of the English upper class for persons in trade may have been less marked at the beginning of the eighteenth century than it was at the beginning of the twentieth.

Voltaire liked to think that the efficacy of inoculation against smallpox was discovered by the Circassians who supplied women to Turkish and Persian harems, so that it was in their commercial interest that these women's beauty should not be marred. He also allowed the possibility that the practice was of Arabian origin. What is not in dispute is that it was introduced into England by Lady Mary Wortley Montagu who came to know of it when she was living in Turkey as wife of the British Ambassador in the reign of George I. It was taken up by the Princess of Wales, afterwards Queen Caroline, the wife of George II, and so became fashionable, though there were clergymen who preached against it as flying in the face of Providence. The assertion made by 'Democritus' in the *Grub Street Journal* of 1733 that 'the doctrines of the Bowstring and of Inoculation in the Small Pox are both of Mahometan origine and can never suit a freeborn English Constitution' may just possibly be ironical. Whether for a similar reason or some other the practice had made no headway in France, where, according to Voltaire, who advocated it strongly in his eleventh letter, it could have saved the lives of the twenty thousand persons who died in Paris in a smallpox epidemic in 1723. This figure is almost certainly an exaggeration.

From the practice of medicine Voltaire turned abruptly to philosophical theory. The next two letters were devoted respectively to Francis Bacon and to John Locke, or Mr Loke, as Voltaire also called him; the next one to a comparison of Descartes and Newton; and the following three to different aspects of Newton's physics, the system of attraction, his theory of optics and his treatment of the infinite and the chronology of the earth.

Francis Bacon, Baron Verulam and Earl of St Albans, who held the office of Lord Chancellor before he was deprived of it in 1621 for taking bribes, was admired by Voltaire chiefly for his *Novum Organum*, an outline of the method he proposed to follow in constructing his complete 'Science of Nature', a work in six parts which his death in 1626 at the age of sixty-five prevented him from completing. Voltaire called Bacon the father of experimental philosophy, not without justice if 'philosophy' is understood in a more modern sense than it usually was by Voltaire. At the same time he could not resist remarking that such astonishing discoveries as those of the compass, printing, engraving, oil-painting, spectacles, and gunpowder preceded the formulation of Bacon's methods, while things even more necessary than printing and the compass, the discovery of fire, the art of making bread, of casting and working metals, of building houses, the invention of the shuttle, were due to men who were still savages. In short, we owe more to a mechanical instinct which most men possess than to a sound philosophy. He was willing, however, to credit Bacon with the discovery of the elasticity of air, with coming near to forestalling Torricelli in the discovery of its weight, and with anticipating Newton at least in sketching the outlines of a theory of gravitation.

John Locke was born in 1632 and died in 1704. His famous *Essay Concerning Human Understanding* was published in 1690 though an abridged version of it, translated into French, had appeared in 1688 in Leclerc's *Bibliothèque Universelle*. Voltaire had surely read this abridgement and probably also the complete Essay in English. He did not refer in his letter on Mr Loke to Locke's *Two Treatises of Government* or his *Letter Concerning Toleration*, though except for Locke's being more hesitant in the domain of religious toleration, the views expressed in them coincided substantially with Voltaire's own.

Voltaire seems to have accepted Locke's Essay *in toto* without reservation, and employed his work mainly as a stick with which to beat earlier philosophers. Taking his cue from Pierre Bayle, whose sceptical *Dictionnaire historique et critique* had been published in 1697, he made short work of all ancient and medieval philosophers, in order to pounce upon Descartes, of whom he said that he had uncovered the errors of antiquity only to substitute his own. The theories of Descartes, who lived from 1596 to 1650, had acquired immense authority in France and it suited Voltaire's iconoclasm to make them appear ridiculous. Thus whereas Locke maintained, to Voltaire's satisfaction, that all our ideas, the materials of reason and knowledge, come to us from Experience, Descartes had argued that some ideas are innate, in the sense that they do not depend on external stimuli. Encouraged by Locke, Voltaire construed this as the absurd theory that 'the soul comes into the body equipped with every metaphysical notion, knowing God, space, infinity, possessing every abstract idea, in short full of splendid pieces of knowledge, which it unfortunately forgets on leaving its mother's womb.' This is not to say that Descartes was right on this point against Locke, but if his position is to be attacked, it is rather on the score of its triviality than its manifest absurdity. There is no doubt that children have innate capacities for learning.

Voltaire objected to Descartes's dualism, according to which the mind is a thinking substance and matter is identified with spatial extension. His view, which was also Locke's, is that this theory fails on both counts. It is empirically false that men's minds are always conscious and even the assumption that matter is unconscious, let alone its resolution into geometry, is open to doubt. There is no ground for denying God the power to annex consciousness to a material organism. No doubt it amused Voltaire to trump Descartes by making his own position appear the more favourable to Theism. We shall see that this was a manoeuvre that he was to repeat. Moreover there is the case of animals, other than men, to be considered. Locke believed them to lack the power of framing abstract ideas, but did not deny them sensation and some form of reason. In view of the consequences, in his system, of crediting animals with consciousness, Descartes had to adopt the implausible thesis that they were machines. It is true that some contemporary philosophers believe men to be machines, but the accomplishments of computers have changed the concept of a machine from what it was in the seventeenth century.

In the letter in which he first compares him to Newton, Voltaire was much kinder to Descartes than he had been in contrasting his philosophy with Locke's. He now does justice to Descartes's eminence as a mathematician and while giving a rough account of the very large differences between Descartes's and Newton's systems of physics does not opt for either. It is only in the following letters on Newton's system of attraction and his optics that Voltaire comes down decisively on Newton's side. One reason for this may be that when he wrote the first letter, in 1728, as may be inferred from his saying that it was written a year after Newton's death, he had read no more than a French review of Newton's *Principia Mathematica*. This would imply that he had not yet read Dr Henry Pemberton's book *A view of Sir Isaac Newton's philosophy* which also came out in 1728, and the passages in which Voltaire expounds Newton in these later letters are taken almost word for word from Pemberton's book. There is no evidence in any of these letters that he had read Newton in the original.

This omission may have been remedied by 1738 when Voltaire published his *Éléments de la philosophie de Newton*. What is curious about this work is that Voltaire maintained in it that Newton's atomic view of matter and his consequent admission of the possibility of a vacuum is consistent with theism, whereas Descartes's equation of matter with extension is not. Voltaire's ground for this opinion was that Descartes's theory makes matter infinite. He did not attempt to show, however, that spatial entails temporal infinity, and anyhow Voltaire's acceptance, in which he followed Newton, of the argument from design, would put the deity outside space and time. I do not say that this deistic hypothesis is intelligible, but only that Voltaire assented to it.

Voltaire had touched on the subject of infinity in the seventeenth of his philosophical letters, with an appendix in which he glanced at earlier approaches to it. He ends by giving Newton precedence over Leibniz in the discovery of the differential calculus and precedence over Jacques Bernoulli in that of the integral calculus. Most of this letter, however, is devoted to an aberration of Newton's, a putative proof, on historical and astronomical grounds, that the voyage of the Argonauts, and consequently the creation of the world, occurred five hundred years later than was commonly believed. This neglect of geological evidence, even on the part of so great a man as Newton, reminds us that we are still dealing with the early part of the eighteenth century.

It is a characteristic of Voltaire that in a second appendix devoted to a sketch of Newton's life he concludes by saying that Newton owed his Mastership of the Mint not to his scientific achievements but to the attraction which his niece Mrs Conduit, or Miss Barton as she then was, awakened in the Lord Treasurer, Lord Halifax.

Up to this point, in every theme which he has explored in his letters, in the spheres of religion, politics, medicine, philosophy and science Voltaire has argued for the superiority of England over France. It is only when he comes to the theatre, and in particular to tragedy, that the order is reversed. The only French tragedians whom he mentions are Corneille and, in a footnote, Racine, of whom he says that his great works, like Virgil's in Latin, were the first to display impeccable taste. We know, however, that he himself was already being hailed as the successor to Corneille and as his career progressed he came to think of himself, and to be widely admired, as superior to any English dramatist, and at least the equal of Racine.

Conformably to the general plan of the letters, Voltaire is concerned to introduce English dramatists to his readers and among them, not surprisingly, he gives pride of place to Shakespeare. After almost a century of neglect, Shakespeare's plays had come back into fashion, largely as a result of the publication of Pope's edition of them. Their revival in the eighteenth century is sometimes attributed to Garrick, but Garrick was born only in 1717, and already, at the end of the 1720s, during Voltaire's stay in England, the performances of Shakespeare's plays in the London theatres were not far short in number of those of all other playwrights put together. Voltaire makes a passing reference to Dryden, whom he allows to have written some good lines of poetry, but otherwise the only plays that he mentions are Otway's *Venice Preserv'd*, which shocked him by its buffoonery and Addison's *Cato*, which he rates very highly. I quote from the original English translation of the eighteenth *Lettre philosophique*, only modernizing the spelling:

> The first English writer who composed a regular tragedy and infused a Spirit of Elegance through every part of it was the illustrious Mr Addison. His *Cato* is a master-piece both with regard to the diction, and the beauty and harmony of the numbers. The character of Cato is, in my opinion, vastly superior to that of Cornelia in the *Pompey* of Corneille. For Cato is great without any thing like fustian, and Cornelia, who besides is not a necessary character, tends sometimes to bombast. Mr Addison's Cato appears to me the greatest character that was ever brought upon any stage, but then the rest of them don't correspond to the dignity of it. And this dramatic piece so excellently well writ, is disfigured by a dull love-plot, which spreads a certain languor over the whole, that quite murders it.

Joseph Addison who lived from 1672 to 1719 and helped to found *The Spectator* in 1711, is still valued for his prose essays, but the verdict of posterity has been that his *Cato*, for whatever reason, has not been worth revival.

What then did Voltaire think of Shakespeare? He was torn between admiration for his genius and contempt for his barbarity. In later years, when versions of Shakespeare's plays by other authors began to appear on the French stage, Voltaire was inclined to lay greater stress upon what he conceived to be Shakespeare's faults, but he never departed very far from the opinion which he expressed succinctly at the beginning of his letter 'Sur la Tragédie'. I quote a slightly more accurate version of the original English translation:

> The English as well as the Spaniards were possessed of theatres, at a time when the French had no more than moving, itinerant stages. Shakespeare, who was considered as the English Corneille, was roughly contemporary with Lopez de Vega, and he created, as it were, the English theatre. Shakespeare boasted a strong fruitful genius. He was natural and sublime, but had not so much as a single spark of good taste, or knew one rule of the drama. I will hazard a bold but true reflection. Which is that this author's merit has ruined the English theatre. There are such beautiful, such noble, such dreadful scenes in his monstrous farces, which go under the name of tragedies, that their performance has always met with great success.

What Voltaire chiefly objected to in Shakespeare, apart from his disregard of the classical unities of place, time and action, a point to which I shall return, was his failure to sustain the nobility of tragedy, his allowing tradesmen to bandy jokes with tribunes in *Julius Caesar*, whereas in his own *La Mort de César* no one less than a senator is allowed to play even a minor role, his admitting the scene of the gravediggers into *Hamlet*, the bawdiness which disfigures nearly all his tragedies, the homeliness of much of his imagery. For example, Voltaire was indignant at a critic's preference for the soldier Francisco's 'Not a mouse stirring' in the opening scene of *Hamlet* to Racine's line from the opening of *Iphigénie*, 'Mais tout dort, et l'armée, et les vents, et Neptune.'

To show how far Voltaire was prepared to go in emasculating Shakespeare I will quote fourteen lines from Shakespeare's famous 'To be or not be be' soliloquy in the third act of *Hamlet* and Voltaire's free rendering of them:

> For who would bear the whips and scorns of time,
> The oppressor's wrong, the proud man's contumely,
> The pangs of despis'd love, the law's delay,

> The insolence of office, and the spurns
> That patient merit of the unworthy takes,
> When he himself might his quietus make
> With a bare bodkin? Who would these fardels bear,
> To grunt and sweat under a weary life,
> But that the dread of something after death –
> The undiscover'd country from whose bourn
> No traveller returns – puzzles the will;
> And makes us rather bear those ills we have,
> Than fly to others that we know not of?
> Thus conscience does make cowards of us all;

And now for Voltaire's rendering. The 'toi' in the first line follows an apostrophe to death:

> Et qui pourrait sans toi supporter cette vie
> De nos Prêtres menteurs bénir l'hipocrisie;
> D'une indigne maîtresse encenser les erreurs,
> Ramper sous un Ministre, adorer ses hauteurs,
> Et montrer les langueurs de son âme abattue,
> A des amis ingrats qui détournent la vue.
> La mort serait trop douce en ces extrémités
> Mais le scruple parle et nous crie, Arrêtez;
> Il défend à nos mains cet heureux homicide,
> Et d'un Héros guerrier, fait un chrétien timide,

The lines scan, the rhymes are correct, but the force of the original has disappeared.

In his discourse on Tragedy, dedicated to Lord Bolingbroke, and published as a preface to his tragedy of *Brutus*, Voltaire complained of the difficulty of resuming his career as a French dramatist after his devoting himself for so long to the study of English literature. What chiefly frightened him, he said, was the severity of French poetry and its subjection to rhyme.

> I regretted the happy freedom which you enjoy to write your tragedies in blank verse; to lengthen and still more to shorten nearly all your words; to let one line run over into another and, where necessary,

to coin new terms, which you do not hesitate to accept so long as they are sonorous, intelligible and fulfil a need. A poet, I am accustomed to say, is a free man who subjugates language to his genius; a Frenchman is a slave to rhyme, forced on occasion to devote four verses to the expression of a thought which an Englishman can capture in a single line. An Englishman says what he pleases, a Frenchman only what he can contrive: one runs over a huge course, the other walks in fetters along a slippery and narrow path.

In spite of all that I have been saying and complaining about, we shall never be able to shed the yoke of rhyme; French poetry cannot do without it. There are few inversions in our language; our lines of poetry do not lend themselves to over-running, or only very rarely; our syllables cannot produce an impression of harmony by their long or short stresses; it is only with the aid of versification that our caesuras and numbering of feet can establish the distinction between poetry and prose; that is why French verses have to rhyme.

Voltaire goes on to say that French audiences had been led to expect rhyming by masters like Racine, Corneille and Boileau, and that it would be taken as a sign of weakness in any later dramatist to rid himself of a burden which the great Corneille had carried.

All this by way of showing why it would be a mistake to try to write French tragedies in blank verse. As for their being written in prose, Voltaire dismisses the idea without argument. He is content to say that it would be like substituting a drawing for a painting. He even goes so far as to prescribe rhymed verse for comedies, a practice to which he himself almost always adhered. He supports this view by saying that Molière's prose comedies were put into verse after their author's death, and that this had become the fashionable way of presenting them, not knowing, or choosing to ignore, the fact that this had been done to only one of them with any success, and that not one of the greatest, *Don Juan, ou Le Festin de pierre*.

At a later point in his discourse, Voltaire admits that some of the rules to which French dramatists were subjected such as not strewing the stage with corpses, or allowing more than three speakers in a scene, were matters of taste and to some extent arbitrary, but he will allow no tampering with the three unities, which he calls the fundamental rules of the theatre. These rules were incorrectly traced back to Aristotle and imposed on the French theatre by Corneille. Voltaire's defence of them is rhetorical. 'It would', he says, 'be feeble and sterile to prolong an action beyond the length of time and the place that suits it. Ask anyone who has crowded too many events into a play the reason for this blemish; if he is honest, he will tell you that he lacked the skill to fill up his play with a single plot; if he requires two days and two towns for his action, believe me that it is because he was not clever enough to confine it within the space of three hours and the enclosure of a palace, as verisimilitude demands.'

Dr Johnson's demolition of the case for two of the three unities, in his preface to his edition of Shakespeare is so splendid that I cannot resist quoting it in full:

> The necessity of observing the unities of time and place arises from the supposed necessity of making the drama credible. The critics hold it impossible, that an action of months or years can be possibly believed to pass in three hours; or that the spectator can suppose himself to sit in the theatre, while ambassadors go and return between distant kings, while armies are levied and towns besieged, while an exile wanders and returns, or till he whom they saw courting his mistress should lament the untimely fall of his son. The mind revolts from evident falsehood, and fiction loses its force when it departs from the resemblance of reality.
>
> From the narrow limitation of time necessarily arises the contraction of place. The spectator, who knows that he saw the first act at Alexandria, cannot suppose that he sees the next at Rome, at a distance to which not the dragons of Medea could, in so short a time, have transported him; he knows with certainty that he has not changed his place; and he knows that place cannot change itself; that what was a house cannot become a plain; that what was Thebes can never be Persepolis.
>
> Such is the triumphant language with which a critic exults over the misery of an irregular poet, and exults commonly without resistance or reply. It is time therefore to tell him, by the authority of Shakespeare, that he assumes, as an unquestionable principle, a position, which, while his breath is forming it into words, his understand-

ing pronounces to be false. It is false, that any representation is mistaken for reality; that any dramatic fable in its materiality was ever credible, or, for a single moment, was ever credited.

The objection arising from the impossibility of passing the first hour at Alexandria, and the next at Rome, supposes, that when the play opens, the spectator really imagines himself at Alexandria, and believes that his walk to the theatre has been a voyage to Egypt, and that he lives in the days of Antony and Cleopatra. Surely he that imagines this may imagine more. He that can take the stage at one time for the palace of the Ptolemies, may take it in half an hour for the promontory of Actium. Delusion, if delusion be admitted, has no certain limitation; if the spectator can be once persuaded, that his old acquaintances are Alexander and Caesar, that a room illuminated with candles is the plain of Pharsalia, or the banks of Granicus, he is in a state of elevation above the reach of reason, or of truth, and from the heights of empyrean poetry, may despise the circumscriptions of terrestrial nature. There is no reason why a mind thus wandering in ecstasy should count the clock, or why an hour should not be a century in that calenture of the brains that can make the stage a field.

The truth is that the spectators are always in their senses, and know, from the first act to the last, that the stage is only a stage, and that the players are only players. They come to hear a certain number of lines recited with just gesture and elegant modulation. The lines relate to some action and an action must be in some place; but the different actions that complete a story may be in places remote from each other: and where is the absurdity of allowing that space to represent first Athens, and then Sicily, which was always known to be neither Sicily nor Athens, but a modern theatre?

This is Dr Johnson at his pungent best, even if he does overstate his case. He attributes too much detachment to the spectator. He does not sufficiently allow for what Coleridge happily called one's 'suspension of disbelief'. Even so, the point which he was concerned to make is sound. Our power of suspending disbelief has no difficulty in accommodating disunities of space and time.

I take it as proved that as a writer of tragedies Voltaire submitted himself to unnecessary handicaps. It does not follow that his tragedies were bad. Racine produced masterpieces while observing all the conventions which Corneille had imposed upon the French theatre. Voltaire and many of his contemporaries believed that the same was true of him, but they were mistaken. Voltaire's tragedies were melodramas and like over-cooked soufflés they have fallen flat.

Apart from Gibbon's favourite, *L'Orphelin de la Chine*, the only one of Voltaire's tragedies that has, to my knowledge, been thought worthy of production on the Paris stage in this century is *Zaire*. Let me summarize its plot. Its setting is the Seraglio of Jerusalem in the thirteenth century at the time of the Sixth Crusade. The setting is constant. The division of scenes is marked by the appearance of a new character on the stage. If a character is soliloquizing, a scene may consist of no more than two lines.

Act I, five scenes. Zaire and Fatima are Christian slaves in the harem of Orosmane, the Sultan of Jerusalem. Zaire has been there since infancy and brought up as a Mahometan. She confesses her love for Orosmane who has respected her virtue, returns her love and intends to marry her. Zaire and Fatima talk of a Frenchman Nérestan who has shared their captivity from childhood and been allowed to leave Jerusalem on his promising to return with a ransom for ten Christian knights. Three scenes later Nérestan reappears with enough money to ransom not only the ten knights, but Zaire and Fatima. Orosmane offers to release a hundred knights, but not Zaire or Lusignan, a Prince of the blood of the Christian kings of Jerusalem, who has been confined in a dungeon for many years. Corasmin, Orosmane's favourite officer, suggests to Orosmane that Nérestan may have designs on Zaire.

Act II, four scenes. Chatillon, one of the liberated knights, expresses his gratitude to Nérestan and bemoans the fate of Lusignan. Zaire arrives and tells them that she has persuaded Orasmane to release Lusignan. Lusignan, by now very old and feeble, speaks of the death of two of his sons, and wonders what has become of his third son and his daughter who were infants when he was captured. He recognizes Zaire as his daughter by a cross that she is wearing and Nérestan as his son by a scar on his chest. There is general rejoicing. Lusignan, fearing Orosmane's anger, makes

Zaire promise not to tell him what they have discovered.

Act III, seven scenes. Orosmane tells Corasmin that he has no fear of Louis IX, who anyhow is busy attacking Egypt. Neither does he fear that the release of Lusignan will put new heart into the Christians. Being a Scythian by birth and not an Asiatic, he will not forbid Zaire to see Nérestan again before Nérestan leaves. When their interview takes place, Nérestan tells Zaire that Lusignan has died of joy at recovering his children, persuades his sister that as a Christian she cannot marry Orosmane, and promises to contrive to have her baptized. Left alone Zaire soliloquizes about the conflict between her new-found faith and her love, ending with the line 'Hélas! et je t'adore, et t'aimer c'est un crime!' Orosmane appears, ready for their wedding. Zaire excuses herself without explaining why. Orosmane, confiding in Corasmin, gives vent to his jealousy and anger.

Act IV, seven scenes. Zaire confides her trouble to Fatima who advises her to keep her secret. Orosmane appears and tells Zaire that he no longer loves her, but weakens when she reveals that she still loves him. Orosmane is perplexed and says so to Corasmin. They are interrupted by an officer who has intercepted a letter from Nérestan to Zaire summoning her to a secret meeting. Corasmin is convinced of Zaire's duplicity and partly persuades Orosmane. When Zaire continues to protest her love for him, Orosmane too is convinced, and swears to be revenged on the ungrateful Christians who have betrayed him.

Act V, ten scenes. Orosmane orders a slave to give Zaire Nérestan's letter and then to spy on her. Fatima persuades Zaire to accede to Nérestan's request. The slave reports this to Orosmane. Orosmane calls for Corasmin and tells him that he is determined on revenge. He surprises Zaire and stabs her to death. Nérestan is brought in chains and a scene ensures of which the following is the high note.

> *Orosmane:* Regarde, elle est ici.
> *Nérestan:* Que dis-tu? Quelle erreur?
> *Orosmane:* Regarde-là, te dis-je.

Nérestan: Ah, que vois-je? Ah, ma soeur! Zaire!... elle n'est plus!
      Ah, monstre! Ah, jour horrible!
Orosmane: Sa soeur! Qu'ai-je entendu? Dieu, serait-il possible?

Orosmane, assured by Fatima that Zaire loved him, then stabs him-self and in the course of dying orders Corasmin to see that all the Christians, including Nérestan, are freed.

Admittedly, it is not fair to judge a tragedy on the mere basis of a summary of its plot. Neither *Othello*, to which *Zaire* is obviously indebted, nor even *Hamlet* would come well out of such a test. The difference is that *Othello* and *Hamlet* are full of fine poetry and dramatic tension, while *Zaire* is not. It contains some gnomic couplets such as:

> J'eusse été près de Gange esclave des faux dieux
> Chrétienne dans Paris, Musselmane en ces lieux.

or

> Non, la reconnaissance est une faible retour
> Un tribut, offensant, trop peu fait pour l'amour.

and some epigrammatic lines which lose nothing by being translated into English: 'One cannot desire what one does not know'; 'I should think myself hated, if I were feebly loved'; 'The most innocent artifice smacks of perfidy'; but nothing profound or sublime.

If this is the best, or among the best, of Voltaire's tragedies, how did it come about that they were so popular? They were full of incident, they tended to combine sly digs at orthodoxy, the versifi-cation was not inflexible, they suited the declamatory style of acting that was then in vogue. As Lytton Strachey put it, commenting on *Mérope:* 'Its glittering was the outcome of no inward fire, but of a certain adroitness in the manufacture; to use our modern phras-eology, Voltaire was able to make up for his lack of genius by a thorough knowledge of "technique" and a great deal of "go".'[1] I consider this a fair verdict on Voltaire's tragedies as a whole.

[1]'Voltaire's Tragedies', reprinted in *Books and Characters*.

Voltaire judged Shakespeare primarily as an author of tragedies, though he had the opportunity to see at least two of Shakespeare's other plays, *The Tempest* and *The Merry Wives of Windsor*, while he was in London. The authors whom he mentions in his letter on Comedy are Thomas Shadwell, whom Dryden satirized and Voltaire found merely vulgar, in spite of Shadwell's being Poet Laureate from 1688 to 1692, William Wycherley, Sir John Vanbrugh, William Congreve, Sir Richard Steele and Colley Cibber, another strange choice as Poet Laureate, an office which Voltaire described as ridiculous but highly profitable. Colley Cibber held it from 1730 to 1758.

Among these writers Voltaire rightly gave pride of place to Congreve, who had just died in 1728, nearly thirty years after the appearance of *The Way of the World*, the last and best-known of his plays, although it did not meet with the immediate success of *Love for Love*. Voltaire said that Congreve always rigorously observed 'the rules of the theatre', which is not true if the rules include preserving the unity of place. I have already told the story of Voltaire's calling on him.

The only play of which Voltaire summarized the plot in this letter is Wycherley's *The Plain Dealer*, which he believed to have been inspired by Molière's *Le Misanthrope*. He noted, amusingly, that an echo of Molière's *Tartuffe* could not succeed in England, because of the lack of religious hypocrites. For there to be pretenders to piety, there had to be genuinely pious people, of whom England had hardly any. On the other hand, thanks to its philosophy, its liberty and its climate, it had more misanthropists than the rest of Europe put together.

Voltaire himself wrote an emasculated version of *The Plain Dealer*, entitled *La Prude*, which was performed in 1747, not at the Comédie-Française, but at the Duchesse de Maine's private theatre at Sceaux, with Voltaire himself and Madame du Châtelet in the leading parts. It is perhaps the most lively of Voltaire's comedies, which is not saying much. Two others which make quite pleasant reading are *L'Enfant prodigue*, in which the prodigal son is not only restored to fortune but also recaptures the heroine from his pompous and acquisitive younger brother, and *Nanine*, in which a virtuous girl of humble origin, brought up in a noble household, ends by marring her protector, the Count, after an intercepted letter believed by him to have been written to a lover turns out to have been written to her long-lost father. Nanine is a cipher but the character of the Count, his chatterbox of a mother, and a spiteful Baroness who wants to marry him are all well drawn.

Another play of Wycherley's in which Voltaire detected the influence of Molière was *The Country Wife*. He related it to Molière's *L'École des femmes*, though the licence enjoyed by playwrights in the reign of Charles II allowed Wycherley a grossness which was forbidden to Molière. While he thought that his plots were inferior to Wycherley's, Voltaire found Vanbrugh's even more amusing. Besides being the author of *The Relapse* and *The Provok'd Wife*, Vanbrugh was also the architect of the Duke of Marlborough's palace of Blenheim, which was thought at the time to be disproportionately grand. Voltaire alluded in prose to Vanbrugh's epitaph, written by a Dr Evans:

> Under this stone, reader, survey
> Dead Sir John Vanbrugh's house of clay
> Lie heavy on him, earth, for he
> Laid many heavy loads on thee

After a letter in praise of the Earl of Rochester, of whose *Homo Sapiens* Voltaire provided a very free translation, and of Edmund Waller, a poet whom Dr Johnson also admired – this being one of the few opinions which he shared with Voltaire, another being their common conviction that *Ossian* was a forgery – Voltaire proceeded to pay tribute to Samuel Butler for his *Hudibras*, of which he freely translated a sample, reducing its first four hundred lines to eighty; to Dean Swift, whom he compared with Rabelais to Swift's advantage; and above all to Alexander Pope, again freely translating a passage from *The Rape of the Lock*. He rightly considered Pope, who lived until 1744, to be the foremost living English poet at the time when the letter was written.

As a Roman Catholic, Pope could not hold office in England but Voltaire cited the large sum of money which Pope received for his translation of Homer as an example of the greater consideration paid to the arts and sciences in England than in France. So, Addison was a Secretary of State, Congreve enjoyed the sinecure of the Secretaryship for Jamaica, Swift had his Deanery in Ireland, Newton did not owe it to his niece that he received a magnificent funeral, with leading members of the Royal Society bearing his coffin to its burial in Westminster Abbey. What particularly impressed Voltaire was that the honour of burial in Westminster Abbey was also accorded to the actress Mrs Oldfield. He contrasted this with the French denial of even a decent burial to Adrienne Lecouvreur.

Voltaire's enthusiasm for English patronage of the arts went so far as to allow him to condone the savage punishment inflicted by the Star Chamber in the reign of Charles I on William Prynne, a barrister, who was condemned to stand twice in the pillory and lose both his ears, besides paying a large fine to the king and suffering imprisonment, for the publication of his *Histrio-Mastyx*, described by David Hume as 'an enormous quarto of a thousand pages'. 'Its professional purpose', wrote Hume, 'was to decry stage-plays, comedies, interludes, music, dancing: but the author likewise took occasion to declaim against hunting, public festivals, Christmas-keeping, bonfires and Maypoles.'[1]

Voltaire might have taken a different view if he had known or recalled that part of Prynne's offence was his attacking Archbishop Laud, but even this is doubtful, since he mocked Prynne for believing that he would be damned if he wore a cassock instead of a short coat and for his supposed wish to see one half of mankind massacre the other for the greater glory of God. Hume, as always, was judicious and humane:

This same Prynne [he wrote] was a great hero among the Puritans; and it was chiefly with a view of mortifying that sect, that, though of an honourable profession, he was condemned by the star-chamber to so ignominious a punishment. The thorough-paced Puritans were distinguishable by the sourness and austerity of their manners, and

[1] David Hume, *The History of England* (London, 1825), vol. VI, p. 228.

by their aversion to all pleasure and society. To inspire them with better humour was certainly, both for their own sake and that of the public, a laudable intention in the court; but whether pillories, fines, and prisons were proper expedients for that purpose, may admit of some question.[1]

Voltaire brings the first edition of the *Lettres philosophiques* to a close by some remarks on the relative merits of French and British academies. He wrote that the English had an Academy of Sciences long before the French, though in fact the interval was only one of six years, the Royal Society being founded in 1660 and the Académie des Sciences in 1666. While freely admitting that the *Transactions* of the Royal Society bore witness to a very impressive list of scientific discoveries, Voltaire found fault with the Society for being too lenient in its requirements for membership. If there was such a fault, it was one that was already being corrected at the time that Voltaire wrote. He also criticized the Royal Society for not confining its membership to scientists but also admitting lovers of the arts, and for making its members pay for membership instead of being paid. On the second point, I am inclined to think that the honour itself should be enough; the first has ceased to be even a debatable objection. For many years now, the Royal Society has confined its membership to scientists on a strict interpretation of the term, except for a servile tendency to admit the odd politician who is distinguished neither in science nor in the arts.

While he was critical of the Académie Française, on the ground that it published nothing but the speeches that members made on their election to it, praising their predecessors, Cardinal Richelieu and Louis XII, Voltaire thought it a pity that England had nothing comparable to it. He said that a proposal to found an academy, which would have included such eminent men of letters as Swift, Prior, Congreve, Dryden, Pope and Addison, was set on foot in the reign of Queen Anne, but that the sudden death of the queen, followed by the transfer of power from the Tories to the Whigs who proposed to hang its sponsors, was fatal to the project. The

[1]Ibid., pp. 229–30.

sponsors in question were Robert Harley, the first Earl of Oxford, and Lord Bolingbroke, neither of whom was actually hanged, though Harley underwent imprisonment in the Tower of London and Bolingbroke, as we have seen, enjoyed rather than suffered a period of exile in France, but this project fell with them and was not revived. When England acquired a Royal Academy in 1768, its purpose was only to found a national school of painting, sculpture and design. A remote analogue to the Académie Française might be the British Academy, designed for scholars in the humanities, which came into being as late as 1902. So far, however, from being limited to forty, the number of its Ordinary Fellows at the last count exceeded four hundred and fifty. I therefore think it more accurate to conclude that a British equivalent to the Académie Française still does not exist.

3

Contra Pascal and Maupertuis

The edition of the *Lettres philosophiques*, which appeared in France in 1734, was enriched by Voltaire's comments on the *Pensées* of Pascal. Blaise Pascal, an excellent scientist and mathematician, who lived from 1623 to 1662, is generally held to have been the originator of the mathematical theory of probability. He was also deeply religious and in 1656–7 composed the *Lettres provinciales* in defence of the Jansenists against the Jesuits, the principal difference between them being that the Jansenists upheld, while the Jesuits rejected, the doctrine of predestination. Pascal's *Pensées* were posthumously published in 1670. Voltaire picked out sixty-five of them for criticism, and added eight more in a note to which he assigned the date 10 May 1738. It would be tedious to reproduce this whole discussion in full, but I believe it to be of sufficient interest to summarize point by point. I shall occasionally add a comment of my own.

(1) P. In view of the heights to which men rise and the depths to which they sink, true religion teaches that they must be governed by two opposing principles, and it should explain how this comes about.

V. This is a false and dangerous approach. Christianity teaches only simplicity, kindness and charity. To try

64

to reduce it to metaphysics is deliberately to plunge it into error.

Already in this first exchange we come upon a fundamental disagreement which is going to run through the entire argument. Pascal is committed to finding a religious explanation for the condition of man. Voltaire's deism allows him to treat Christianity as nothing more than a moral code. Voltaire may well be right in thinking that the metaphysical aspects of Christianity are false, or even nonsensical, but it is disingenuous of him to pretend that there are no such aspects, and thereby hoist Pascal with his own petard, as we shall see that he proceeds to do.

(2) P. Christianity is the only satisfactory religion. Philosophers who locate the ground of goodness in ourselves fall into the error either of elevating mankind to God or reducing it to the beasts.

V. Philosophers do not come into it. What needs to be shown is that Christianity is true and that Mahometanism, Paganism, and other religions are false. Christ is not in competition with Aristotle.

(3) P. The mystery of our condition is knotted in the abyss of original sin. Man is more inconceivable without this mystery than this mystery is inconceivable to man.

V. Rubbish. Why try to improve on Scripture? There is no mystery about what a man is. He comes into the world like other animals which he resembles organically. There are natural explanations for the disparities in human intelligence and character. God has given us self-love for our own preservation, and religion to govern our self-love. Man has his proper position in nature, superior to animals, inferior to other beings, whom he probably resembles in his capacity for thought.

It is surprising to find Voltaire admitting the existence of these other beings, presumably angels. Perhaps he felt that he was committed to it by his championship of Scripture.

(4) P. Man is so full of contradictions that he is surely not a simple subject. We have two natures and there are those who think that we have two souls.

V. Our different acts of will are not contradictions. Of course, man is not a simple subject. He is composed of a countless number of organs, the actions of which in varying environments account for the differences in his thoughts, his sentiments and his behaviour. It is as ridiculous to credit him with a double nature, as it would be to credit a dog with a double nature because it sometimes licks you and sometimes bites, or a tree because it both displays and sheds its leaves.

(5) P. Not to bet on the existence of God is to bet against it. But you should bet on it. For in so doing you have everything to gain, and nothing to lose. Suppose that the chances are even, you are still betting on having two lives against one.

V. It is false that failure to bet on the existence of God is to bet against it. One can be genuinely agnostic. To reduce it to betting is to trivialize the issue. Moreover its being in one's interest to believe that something exists is not a proof that it does exist. Worse still, it is not even in one's interest to believe that God exists if Pascal and his friends are right in thinking that only one person in a million is saved. Pascal gives ammunition to atheists. The proof of the existence of God lies in the organization of nature.

Voltaire's point about self-interest is decisive *ad hominem*. If salvation or the lack of it is predestined, it does not matter how one bets, and if the vast majority who are not saved are damned one should reasonably hope that the whole business is a fiction. There is no force in Pascal's argument unless one assumes that one will be rewarded for placing one's bet on God's existence, and that, indeed, is how it has generally been construed. Even so, there is the objection that one's beliefs are subject to one's reason. I doubt if it is psychologically possible to believe both that some proposition is true and that there are no rational grounds for believing it, however much its truth would be to one's advantage. A further point is that the prize for winning the bet, according to Pascal, is a future life and it is not self-evident that a future life would be any improvement on the present. Professor Broad, for example, thought that the chances were that it would be more unpleasant, though he also thought, on the evidence of psychical research, that he stood an even chance of surviving his death in some fashion or other.[1]

Bertrand Russell's reaction to Pascal's wager is worth recording. He argued that if there were a just God, he would expect men to make proper use of the reason with which he had endowed them. Since he had not supplied them with sufficient evidence for believing in his existence, he would be displeased with those who did so and pleased with those who did not. Russell made this not wholly serious point to me in conversation. I do not know if he ever put it into print.

For my own part I agree with Russell, and with Kant before him, in rejecting both the cosmological argument for the existence of God and the argument from design. Unlike Voltaire, I see no good reason to believe either that the Universe had a supernatural cause, or that it serves any purpose.

(6) P. The condition of men on earth, not knowing who put them there, or for what reason, or what will happen to them after death is as wretched as that of a man marooned on a desert island. It is astonishing that we are not all in a state of constant despair.

V. Not all men are miserable. Paris and London are not like desert islands. To look upon the Universe as a gaol and men as criminals condemned to execution is the idea of a fanatic. To think of the world as a paradise in which one experiences nothing but pleasure is the

[1] Cf. C.D.Broad, *Lectures on Psychical Research* (London, 1962).

dream of a sybarite. Men are as happy as they deserve to be.

(7) P. The Jews believe that God will not allow the rest of mankind to languish eternally in darkness; that they are the people chosen to announce the arrival of man's liberator and to form a union to await him.

V. The Jews do indeed expect a Messiah, but they expect him to give them power over Christians. We, on the other hand, look to the Messiah to reunite Jews and Christians.

If Voltaire was referring to the Jews of the Old Testament, he was right historically. That was one of the reasons for his outbursts of anti-Semitism. It is interesting that he too appears to put the coming of the Messiah into the future.

(8) P. Jewish law is the oldest in the world. The Greeks and Romans took their laws from it.

V. Both propositions are false. The laws of Egypt are older. The Greek and Roman republics had no commerce with the Jews.

(9) P. The Jews are to be admired for their fidelity to Moses and their promotion of the Old Testament, which records their offences against God. Such sincerity is unexampled and is not rooted in nature.

V. There are many examples and they are rooted only in nature. It suits a Jew's pride to believe that his misfortunes are due not to his detestable politics, his ignorance of the arts and his coarseness but to the anger of God.

It may be that Voltaire was referring only to the Jews as the Old Testament depicts them. If he was referring to his Jewish contemporaries, then not only has he misrepresented their character but he has ignored the effect on them of centuries of Christian persecution.

(10) P. If there is a God, we should love him only, and not his creatures.

V. A barbarous proposition. One should love one's country, one's wife, one's father, one's children, and God should see to it that we do so, in spite of ourselves.

(11) P. We are born unjust, because we are born selfish. Selfishness is the source of all disorder. We should aim at the general good.

V. Quite the contrary. Self-interest promotes benevolence. The law regulates it and religion perfects it.

I believe that Hume was nearer the mark in crediting us with an innate principle of sympathy besides a principle of egoism.

(12–15) P. and V. dispute about Old and New Testament prophecies. P. says that the first coming of Christ was ambiguously predicted, the second not at all. V. says the second coming was clearly, though falsely predicted, and that one should not impute ambiguity to God's utterances. The Jews could not have been expected to detect a Messiah in Jesus and anyhow their hope for a liberator was not an element in their religion.

(16) P. The infinite distance of bodies from spirits represents the infinitely greater distance of spirit from charity, for it is supernatural.

V. Pascal's editors did him a disservice in printing such nonsense.

(17) P. To the initiated apparent weaknesses are strengths. For example, the fact that the genealogies of St Matthew and St Luke are mutually inconsistent proves that they did not concert their evidence.

V. Odd that contradiction should be taken as a mark of truth.

(18) P. The truth of religion consists in its obscurity.

V. Come, come.

(19) P. If there were only one religion, God would be too manifest.

V. Why then is Pascal going to all this trouble to try to make God manifest?

(20) P. The Jewish religion consisted only in the love of God and God reprehended everything else.

V. What about all the commandments that the Old Testament attributed to God?

(21) P. The choice of a profession is the most important thing in life. It is subject to chance and custom.

V. So what? It is only in works of genius that we find self-determination.

Both parties shirk the problem of free will.

(22) P. Our thought is concerned only with the past and future, hardly ever with the present, and then only with an eye to the future.

V. Not altogether true, and anyhow we do well to take thought for the future.

(23–8) P. discourses on the misery of man, says that true happiness consists in being calm, ends by remarking that men are easily diverted from their sorrow. V. says that men are made for action. Calm produces boredom. It is a good thing that men are not overcome by sorrow.

(29) P. Wise men among the Pagans were persecuted for their monotheism, the Jews hated, the Christians even more so.

V. Socrates was put to death not for his monotheism but for his alleged impiety and for political reasons. The Jews were hated for their aggressiveness, their barbarity and for despising people more civilized than themselves. As for the Christians, they were hated by the pagans for undermining the Roman empire. In the same way, Protestants were hated, persecuted and slaughtered in the countries of which they eventually became masters.

Voltaire's hatred and contempt for the Jews of the Old Testament may have been reinforced by a so far unavowed hostility to Christianity, viewed as an outcrop of Judaism.

(30) P. There are great faults in Montaigne. His advocacy of suicide is particularly offensive.

V. Montaigne writes as a philosopher not a Christian. He sets out the arguments for and against suicide fairly and he reaches the rational conclusion that there are circumstances in which suicide is justified.

(31) P. People were mistaken in attacking Holy Scripture for exaggerating the number of stars.

V. So far as physics is concerned Scripture accepted the beliefs current at the time, for instance that the earth is flat, that the sun moves etc. God never revealed that Flamsteed with the aid of his telescope would catalogue more than seven thousand stars.

Assuredly, he never revealed the astronomical discoveries of the twentieth century.

(32) P. Is it courageous for a dying man to set out in his weakness and agony to confront an omnipotent and eternal God?

V. This has never happened. Only in a state of madness would a man say 'I believe in a God and I defy him'.

John Stuart Mill said that he would go to Hell for his beliefs, but he did not believe in a God who would send him there.

(33) P. I am ready to believe stories when those who vouch for them allow themselves to be martyred.

71

V. Whether a witness is credible depends not on his readiness to suffer martyrdom, which is true of many fanatics, but on his being in a position to know the truth of what he asserts. How is it that Josephus who fulfils this condition in the case of Jesus fails to mention him?

(34) P. The sciences trace a circle. Man is born ignorant and the wisest men end by discovering that they know nothing.

V. Sophistry. The fact that a mathematician does not know the hidden principles of nature does not make him an ignoramus.

(35) P. Enjoying entertainment is not happiness. For it comes from outside oneself and it is insecure.

V. A man is happy if he is in a state of pleasure. But pleasure comes from external objects, like all our sensations and ideas. Food is external and we could not live without it.

(36) P. The exaltation of the spirit, like the total lack of it, gets taken for madness. Only mediocrity passes for goodness.

V. It is not the exaltation of the spirit, but its turmoil and volatility that get taken for madness. What passes for goodness is not mediocrity but the just mean between two opposing vices.

Are we to take it that Voltaire himself subscribes to the ethics of Aristotle?

(37) P. If our condition were really happy, we should not try to avoid thinking about it.

V. Our condition consists in thinking about external objects with which we have a necessary relation. Because of this necessary relation we cannot avoid thinking about the human condition; conversely, we cannot think about ourselves in abstraction from natural things. Besides, men like to have their attention drawn to the amenities of their condition.

Both parties go astray here. Inattention to one's happiness does not impair its genuineness. The fact that our ideas have an external origin does not prevent us from concentrating on them internally. It neither obliges us to think about the human condition in general nor prevents us from doing so. Not all men enjoy being flattered.

(38) P. Great and little people have the same accidental properties, the same arrogance, the same passions. But those near the centre of the wheel are less disturbed by the same movements than those at the top.

V. Little people are more liable to be disturbed because they have fewer resources. Ninety per cent of the suicides in London come from the lower classes. The simile of the wheel is ingenious but false.

Even if Voltaire has got his statistics right, he may have misinterpreted Pascal's simile.

(39) P. Men are not taught to be virtuous, though they are taught everything else. Nevertheless they pride themselves on their virtue, that is on knowing the only thing which they do not learn.

V. Men are taught to be virtuous and they would not be so otherwise. Their behaviour depends on their upbringing.

(40) P. How foolish of Montaigne to try to portray himself. It is common enough for people to talk rubbish, but to do so deliberately!

V. How feeble of Nicole, Malebranche and Pascal to decry Montaigne. In depicting himself Montaigne depicted human nature.

(41) P. Impostors in medicine get away with it only because there are competent doctors. False effects are attributed to the moon only because there are real ones, like the

tides. Similarly there are so many false miracles, revelations, omens, only because there are real ones.

V. Falsehood is not always parasitic on truth. What about the belief in werewolves or in the philosopher's stone?

(42) P. Sailors make for port. What corresponds to this in morality?

V. The single maxim current in all nations 'Do not do to others what you would not like done to yourself.'

This maxim has a reasonable claim to general acceptance, but it is open to Shaw's objection that we do not all have the same tastes.

(43) P. Some people prefer death to peace, others prefer death to war.

V. According to Tacitus the first was true of the Catalans. Nobody prefers death to war.

People who go to war, hope to survive. But self-sacrifice occurs in war.

(44) P. The more intelligent one is, the more one discovers originality among men. To the common people, all men are alike.

V. There are very few really original men. Most men are wholly governed by custom and education. But among the mass who travel along the highway there are differences perceptible to a keen eye.

(45) P. There are two types of intelligence. The logical type that shines at deduction: the geometrical type that comprehends a great number of principles without confusing them.

V. Current usage would call a methodical and consistent intelligence geometrical.

(46) P. Death is easier to bear without thinking of it, than the thought of death without danger.

V. There is no question of its being either easy or difficult to bear death, if one does not think about it at all.

(47) P. We assume that all men have the same concepts and sensations when objects of the same kind are presented to them. For instance they agree in saying that snow is white, but this is not a conclusive proof that their experiences are the same.

V. White has the same effect on all eyes, because it combines all the rays of light. There may be differences in the case of other colours.

Voltaire mistakes a philosophical for a scientific question. Philosophers still disagree about the correct way to deal with the problem of one's knowledge of other minds.

(48) P. All our reasoning consists in giving way to sentiment.

V. In matters of taste, not in science.

(49) P. Those who judge a work by a rule are related to others as those who measure time by a watch are to those who measure it subjectively.

V. In works of taste, music, poetry, painting, taste takes the place of a watch; it is a bad judge who judges them only by rules.

Voltaire would presumably have wished to discriminate between good and bad taste, but throughout the discussion tended to overlook philosophical difficulties.

(50) P. It seems to me that Caesar was too old to take pleasure in conquering the world. It was all right for a young man like Alexander, but Caesar should have been more mature.

V. Neither Caesar nor Alexander planned to conquer the world. They were responding to a series of historical causes. Anyhow Pascal has got it the wrong way round. Caesar needed to be mature to cope with his political problems. It is astonishing that Alexander, at his age, should have renounced pleasure in order to engage in such a dreadful war.

(51) P. It is amusing to reflect that there are people, like thieves, who renounce the laws of God and nature, and yet are strictly bound by their own.

V. It is not so much amusing as instructive. It shows that no human society can last for a day without rules.

(52) P. Man is neither an angel nor a beast. The trouble is that those who want to be angels behave like beasts.

V. The people who want to be angels are those who want to destroy their passions instead of governing them.

(53) P. Men are competitive in ways that horses are not. Virtue in itself does not satisfy them. They want to gain some advantage from it over others.

V. Both among animals and among men, the big devour the small.

(54) P. If men began by studying themselves, they would realize their limitations. They cannot aspire to any knowledge, because parts of the world cannot be known independently of one another, or of the whole.

V. The fact that one cannot know everything does not entail that one cannot know anything.

Voltaire ventures into philosophy and gets it right. It is interesting to find Pascal anticipating one of the main theses of Absolute Idealism and making it a basis for scepticism.

(55) P. If lightning fell in the valleys, poets and their like would lack instances.

V. A simile is not a proof, either in poetry or prose.

(56) P. The mixture of mind and body has led philosophers astray. They ascribe to the body what belongs only to the mind and vice versa.

V. We have no idea of the mind and a very imperfect idea of the body. Consequently, we do not know where to draw the line between them.

As usual, Pascal exaggerates and once again Voltaire declines to tackle a philosophical problem.

(57) P. As one attributes beauty to poetry, so one should attribute it to geometry and medicine. The reason why this does not happen is that the aims of geometry and medicine are known, whereas it is not known in what the charm, which is the aim of poetry, consists. The terms used to praise poetry are mere jargon.

V. The reason why geometry and medicine are not said to be beautiful is that they do not appeal to the senses, as do music, architecture etc. The aim of poetry is to depict things forcefully, precisely, delicately and harmoniously. Poetry is harmonious eloquence. Pascal's account of literary criticism is a travesty.

Mathematicians do talk of beautiful theorems and it may be that doctors talk of beautiful operations. Voltaire's venture into aesthetics is superficial.

(58) P. In society, poets and mathematicians are known by the honours paid to them; but really honest men scorn decorations.

V. Why should people shrink from being known to excel in their profession? Virgil, Homer, Corneille and Newton did not.

(59) P. The common people have very sensible opinions: for instance, they choose entertainment and hunting rather than poetry etc.

V. As if people chose between playing bowls or writing verses! Grosser people seek purely physical pleasures. Those who have more delicate feelings look for subtler pleasures. Everybody must live.

(60) P. If the Universe were to crush a man, the man would be the nobler of the two, because he would know what the Universe was doing to him, which the Universe would not.

V. What does the world 'noble' mean here? What right has a man to judge that he is nobler than the sun? Why should some commonplace idea lodged in a brain rate above the material universe?

On Pascal's side compare F.P.Ramsey: 'The stars may be large but they cannot think or love.'[1]

(61) P. Whatever a man's condition, if one put together all the goods and satisfactions that he could desire and deprived him of occupation and entertainment, he would on reflection find such a state of happiness intolerable.

V. The supposition is self-contradictory.

(62) P. A king, left all alone, with his senses unsatisfied and no food for thought would be as unhappy as anyone else.

V. A king whose only thought was 'I am reigning' would be an idiot.

(63) P. Any religion which does not recognize Jesus Christ is notoriously false and miracles cannot save it.

V. What is a miracle? Something that only God can bring about. Could God work a miracle in aid of a false religion? This would be worth looking into.

It is a pity that Voltaire does not proceed to do so.

(64) P. We are instructed to believe in the Church but not to believe in miracles, because the second is natural and the first not.
Only the first needs an order.

[1] *The Foundations of Mathematics* (London 1931) p. 291.

V. This contradicts Pascal's previous saying.

(65) P. I do not see why it should be more difficult to believe in the resurrection of the body and the Virgin birth than in creation. Is it more difficult to recreate a man than to create him?

V. There is a rational proof of creation, because matter and motion cannot have come into being of their own accord. The other miracles are objects of faith, not reason.

Voltaire's reply depends upon the validity of the cosmological argument.

The short sequel to the foregoing discussion was separated from it in time, not in character.

(1) P. Whenever a proposition is inconceivable, examine its contrary. If the contrary is manifestly false, one can assert *its* contrary, for all its being inconceivable.

V. Contrary propositions may both be false. For example, 'Cattle fly to the South', 'Cattle fly to the North'.

Pascal presumably meant 'contradictory' rather than 'contrary', but the contradictory of an absurd proposition is itself absurd. In such cases, neither calls for acceptance.

(2) P. What a silly business Painting is, expecting us to admire imitations, when we do not admire the original.

V. One admires a portrait for its resemblance to the sitter, not for the sitter's merits.

Pascal's thought is silly. Voltaire's rebuttal need not have been confined to representational pictures. Neither provides a criterion for aesthetics.

(3) P. Doctors of all sorts owe the respect in which they are held to their trappings.

V. Not so.

(4) P. According to our natural lights, if there is a God, he is infinitely incomprehensible, having neither parts, nor limits and no relation to ourselves. We are therefore incapable of knowing what he is, or even if he exists.

V. It is strange that Pascal should have thought that our reason could prove the existence of original sin, but not the existence of God. In effect, we have to admit things that we cannot conceive. 'I exist, therefore something exists from eternity' is a self-evident proposition, but do we understand eternity?

What an extraordinary concession for Voltaire to make. His self-evident proposition seems to me a flagrant non-sequitur.

(5) P. Do you think it impossible that God can be infinite without parts? A point moving everywhere with an infinite velocity, is in all places at once, and whole in each place.

V. Four obvious falsehoods (1) that a mathematical point exists on its own (2) that it moves to left and right at the same time (3) that it moves with an infinite velocity, for any velocity however great can be increased (4) that the point is an omnipresent whole.

There is one place in which Voltaire is out of step with modern physics. It is now held that no velocity can exceed the velocity of light. Even so, this is supposed to be finite.

(6) P. Homer wrote fiction. No one thinks that Troy and Agamemnon really existed, any more than the golden apple.

V. No writer has had any doubt that there really was a Trojan war, even if the story of the golden apple is obviously fictional. All sorts of legends have attached themselves to Clovis, but this does not prevent his having been King of France.

(7) P. I shall not try to prove, by natural theology, either the existence of God, or the Trinity, or the immortality of the Soul, because I should not have the power to discover in

nature sufficient grounds for convincing stubborn atheists.

  V. How strange that such an admission should come from Pascal.

Not but what Pascal is right.

  (8) P. Easy opinions have such a natural hold over men, that it is strange when they fail to convince them.

      V. On the contrary, people like to believe what is mysterious. Endow Divinity with thunderbolts, shed blood on his altars, and the mass of people will say 'He must be right, because he made such strange pronouncements with such confidence.'

Throughout this long debate, Pascal is handicapped, as a Jansenist, by being saddled with an avowedly hidden God. Voltaire almost always has the better of the argument, but one sometimes gets the feeling that he is content to score points too easily. I have sometimes been reminded of the part played in twentieth-century philosophy by G.E.Moore's defence of common sense. This should not, however, be taken to imply that Moore was in any degree a slippery customer.

We have seen that Pierre-Louis Moreau de Maupertuis, a Frenchman who had been made President of the Berlin Academy of Sciences, was Voltaire's chief rival at the court of Frederick the Great. Voltaire would probably have found a pretext for quarrelling with him in any case, but Maupertuis' high-handed treatment of the respectable Professor Koenig gave him a fair opportunity of which we have seen that he took advantage. So far, the provenance of Voltaire's charge was moral. Maupertuis was a better mathematician than Voltaire and knew more physics, but his self-confidence led him to publish some foolish speculations on which Voltaire pounced. The result was the *Diatribe du docteur Akakia* and its sequels, concerning a so-called 'native of St Malo' whose conceit had driven him mad. There had in fact been three generations of doctors, named Akakia, who had successfully practised medicine in Paris in the sixteenth and seventeenth centuries. The character to whom Voltaire attached their name was, of course, fictitious.

La Diatribe, which is not a diatribe, in the English sense of the word, but the parody of a diagnosis, begins with the assumption that Maupertuis' *Letters* are the product of a young impostor, guilty among other things of plagiarizing Maupertuis' *Works*.

For who but an impostor would propose that doctors should not be paid if they fail to cure their patients, just as a painter is not paid for a bad picture. Painters are often paid for bad pictures, just as lawyers are paid when they lose their cases. A doctor is paid for doing his best.

Here we have the case of a man who draws a handsome salary for expounding Mathematics and Metaphysics, for having dissected two toads, and had himself painted in a fur hat. The Treasurer should say to him:

Sir, you must forfeit a hundred ducats for having written that there are stars fashioned like millstones, a hundred more for having written that a comet will come and steal our moon, and venture even to attack our sun, still another hundred for having conjectured that golden and diamond comets will fall to earth: you are fined three hundred ducats for having stated that children are formed by attraction in the mother's womb, and that the left eye attracts the right leg. We cannot allow you to forfeit less than four hundred ducats for having proposed to discover the nature of the soul by means of opium and by dissecting the heads of giants etc. etc.

In the end the poor philosopher would be left without any salary at all.

This foolish young man [Dr Akakia continues] accuses my medical colleagues of timidity. He says that all known remedies have a primitive origin or are discovered by chance. He should be made to see that chance needs to be vindicated by experiment, just as experiment needs the support of theory. His suggestion that doctors can dispense with theory is like saying that we can build houses without architects. His own indebtedness to surgeons should have prevented him from saying that doctors need not bother with the study of anatomy.

The same author advocates that experiments should be made on criminals and complains that this has never been done. Here he shows his ignorance of history. Louis XI sanctioned an operation on a condemned criminal; the Queen of England tried out vaccination on four criminals and there are other precedents.

This should be enough to reproduce the flavour of Voltaire's mildly amusing satire. It is rather shocking that he should accept the principle of experiments on criminals and reprove Maupertuis only for ignoring that it had already been put into practice.

In the remainder of the diagnosis, the patient is teased, among other things, for advocating acupuncture and for recommending that doctors should specialize. Voltaire characteristically turns this into the suggestion that if a man is suffering simultaneously from gout, fever, derangement, cataract and earache he should employ five doctors and pay them each a fifth of what he would have paid a general practitioner. The diagnosis ends with the remark that if the letters under review really emanated from a President it could only have been a President of Bedlam.

Voltaire went on to pretend that the *Diatribe* had been submitted to the Inquisition at Rome which had appointed a committee of Professors of Philosophy of the College of Wisdom to examine the issue. In their judgement they condemned Dr Akakia's patient for mis-stating the law of least action, acquitted him of stealing it from Leibniz, since he had stolen only half of it, advised him when he made love not to imitate the action of snails or toads, and condemned him for plagiarizing his own *Works*. There followed an examination of the *Letters* in which the following points are made.

1. The young author must learn not to confuse foresight with precognition, which only God possesses.
2. It is false that we lose more than we gain by memory.
3. We find it ridiculous to suppose that the soul, like the body, returns, after agitation, to its natural state of rest.
4. The candidate is mistaken in saying that extension is only a mental impression. Every schoolboy knows that extension

exists independently of our sensations, unlike sound and colour.

5. The candidate should not libel Germans. He is not altogether wrong but he should be polite.

6. We are afraid that the author may tempt his associates to search for the philosopher's stone.

7. The Inquisitor will be surprised to learn that the young student proposes to dissect the brains of giants who are more than twelve feet high, to fatten eels with flour, to breed fish out of wheat and to engage in other absurdities.

8. The Inquisitor will be even more amused to discover that everyone can be a prophet, for the author claims that it is not more difficult to see into the future than the past.

9. If instead of embarking on a voyage to the Antipodes, which he appears to want to do, the author also carries out his plan of travelling straight to the north pole, or digging a hole to the centre of the earth, no one will accompany him.

10. We ask Dr Akakia to prescribe his patient some refreshing tisanes, and urge the patient to study at a university modestly.

There follow some decrees, in effect rebuking Maupertuis for his tyrannical behaviour towards Koenig.

Of the points listed, the only ones that call for comment are the fourth, in which Voltaire uncritically adopts Locke's position on the question of primary and secondary qualities, and to a lesser extent the first and eighth. Our powers of memory do in fact greatly exceed our powers of precognition, but there is only a causal, not a logical reason for this discrepancy.

The verdict of the committee set up by the Inquisition is followed by a fictitious report of a meeting of the Berlin Academy in which the more outrageous medical suggestions, attributed by Dr Akakia to his patient, are put to the test. The meeting is said to have concluded with an eloquent speech by its permanent secretary, in the course of which he said that only an Erasmus could do justice to the President's merits and went on to raise the President's monad to the skies, or at least to the fog. The President was set beside

Cyrano de Bergerac: a throne of bladders was created for him and he was dispatched to the moon.

The reference to the President's monad is again a way of taunting Maupertuis for his indebtedness to Leibniz, since the theory that the world consisted of simple spirits, called monads, was the central point of Leibniz's metaphysics.

The farce continues with a treaty of peace concluded between the President and the Professors on 1 January 1753. The treaty consists of fifteen articles of which the only one of interest is the eighth in which the President is made to ask God's forgiveness for having claimed that the only proof of his existence consisted in some such formula as A + B divided by Z. It was true that Maupertuis had succumbed to the absurdity of suggesting that the existence of God was susceptible of a purely mathematical proof.

The President is said to have been on the point of signing the treaty when he succumbed to a more violent attack of melancholia and pride. As a result he wrote a letter to Dr Akakia threatening to kill him. Dr Akakia, who was ill at Leipzig, appealed to the Governor for protection. At the same time he wrote to the President saying that he was currently too ill to be able to defend himself with more than a syringe and a chamber-pot, but that he hoped soon to be able to use a pistol. The episode is represented as ending with a letter of Dr Akakia to the permanent secretary of the Berlin Academy, in which he asks whether it is in accordance with the principle of least action that the President should assassinate one of his associates. He says that in order to spare either the President or the secretary the embarrassment of having to pronounce a formal oration over him he offers his resignation before the President kills him.

The satire is good enough in parts, but it is so relentless and repetitive that one comes to feel sympathy for its victim.

4

Voltaire's Conception of History

It is not generally known that Voltaire was a voluminous historian. One of his earliest publications was a history of Charles XII of Sweden who lived from 1682 to 1718 and came to the throne in 1697. His reign was remarkable for the fact that it was almost entirely devoted to the pursuit of war for which Charles had an insatiable passion and an extraordinary aptitude. In nine years of campaigning, almost always with forces inferior in number to those of his opponents, he extended the influence of Sweden over Denmark, all the Baltic states, Poland, and the north of Germany. I speak of the influence rather than the empire of Sweden, because Charles's habit was not so much to annex territory as to install rulers who were subservient to himself. Like other military adventurers, he came to grief in Russia. Having penetrated deep into the Ukraine he was defeated in 1709 at the battle of Poltava by Peter the Great, and forced to take refuge in Turkey, where he vainly attempted to persuade the Sultan to supply him with an army to lead against Russia. In 1714 he reappeared at Stralsund, then still a Swedish outpost on the Baltic, after riding through Hungary, Austria and a large part of Germany in sixteen days, with an escort of only two officers. He spent the next four years in a mainly unsuccessful attempt to restore the fortunes of his country, which had suffered military reverses during his absence, and was killed by a stray cannon-ball while directing the siege of a Norwegian fortress. Charles XII left Sweden the poorer both in influence and territory than when he embarked, at the age of eighteen, upon his career of conquest.

Voltaire told this story well, though it is a little surprising, in view of the number of his other interests, that he should have chosen to tell it at all. What is even more surprising is that the book was considered subversive by the authorities, so that it had to be printed surreptitiously in Rouen. Mr Besterman[1] quotes as evidence a paragraph in the preface to the effect that the only events worth recording are those that have produced great changes, or those that stand out from the mass through being described by some very good writer, like the portraits of obscure men painted by great masters, but this hardly seems sufficient to have alarmed the youthful Louis XV or his ministers, even on Besterman's careless reading of the passage which led him to substitute 'kings' for 'events'. Perhaps it was just assumed, unwarrantably, that anything that Voltaire wrote about a monarch was likely to be irreverent.

In this connection, it is worth quoting Voltaire's summary of Charles's career, if only as a good example of his style of writing history:

So perished, at the age of thirty-six and a half, Charles XII, King of Sweden, having experienced the heights of prosperity and the utmost bitterness of adversity, without being softened by the one or cast down for a moment by the other. Nearly all his actions, consistently with his private life, went far beyond the bounds of probability. He is perhaps the only man, and so far the only king, to have lived without any weakness; he carried all the heroic virtues to a pitch where they became as dangerous as their opposite vices. His strength of will, developed into obstinacy, caused his misfortunes in the Ukraine and kept him for five years in Turkey: his generosity, degenerating into extravagance, ruined Sweden; his courage, swollen into rashness, caused his death: his justice developed sometimes into

[1] See his *Voltaire*, p. 157.

cruelty; and in the last years of his life the maintenance of his authority came near to being tyrannical. His great qualities, of which any single one could have immortalized another prince, were injurious to his country. He never attacked anyone; but he cast aside prudence in his implacable pursuit of revenge. He was the first man to be ambitious for conquest, without desiring to increase his possessions; he wanted to win empires in order to give them away. His passion for glory, for war, and for revenge, prevented him from being a good politician, a quality which no conqueror has ever been seen to lack. Before battle and after victory he was never anything but modest; unfailingly resolute after defeat; hard on others as he was on himself, heedless of the suffering and lives of his subjects as he was of his own; an exceptional rather than a great man, and one to admire rather than to imitate. His life should teach kings how far a peaceful and happy government is superior to such an abundance of glory.

Voltaire's history of Charles XII inevitably overlapped at several points with his subsequent *History of the Russian Empire under Peter the Great* in two volumes, of which the first appeared in 1759 and the second in 1763. The very great enthusiasm which they display for Peter's character and achievements cannot be wholly attributed to Voltaire's friendship with the Empress Catherine II, since we have seen that their correspondence started only in 1762, but this friendship may have been partly responsible for Voltaire's gingerly treatment in the second volume of the blackest episode in Peter the Great's career, his execution in 1718 of his eldest son Alexis on a charge of treason based on very slender evidence. It is to Voltaire's credit that he does put his readers in a position to draw the inference that Peter's actions were not only inhumane but unjust. At the same time Voltaire does not disguise his sympathy for what he conceives to have been Peter's strongest motive: the fear that Alexis, who had succumbed to the influence of Russian priests and had indeed offered to renounce his title to the succession if he were permitted to retire into a monastery, would go back upon his word and having ascended to the throne would allow power to pass into the hands of the patriarchs of the Orthodox Church. Not that Peter the Great believed that the doctrines of the Orthodox Church were less acceptable than those of other forms of Christianity. He took as little interest as Voltaire in the question whether the Holy Ghost proceeds from both the Father and the Son or only from the Father via the Son. His opposition to the Church was political. His primary purpose during the thirty-six years of his effective rule from the time he acquired entire authority in 1689 at the age of seventeen, having reigned for five years under his half-sister Sophia's tutelage, was to turn Russia into a European power, and he feared that unless his successors kept the Church in subordination, its leaders would undo the social reforms by which this purpose had been achieved.

When I speak in this context of social reforms, I do not intend to imply that the condition of the peasantry, which constituted the bulk of the Russian people, was significantly altered in the reign of Peter the Great. He did not alleviate their state of serfdom, diminish the extent of their illiteracy, or relieve them of their superstitious beliefs. Internally, the changes which he effected were those that in earlier centuries had brought such countries as England and France out of the era of feudalism. He divested both the clergy and the nobility of their independent power and subjected them to the control of the central government, which in the case of Russia was, and in theory remained, an absolute monarchy for nearly two hundred years and longer still in practice. Externally, he made Russia a force in Europe, not only by the influence over Poland and the northern states of Germany which he owed to his defeat of Charles XII, but still more by his development of a navy which secured Russia the control of the Baltic. To prepare himself for this he went abroad in 1697 and spent over a year first at Sadom in Holland and then at Deptford in England learning the trade of a shipwright. The account which Voltaire gives of his seriousness in this undertaking and of his supposedly simple standard of living shows him in an attractive light which, unfortunately, is not sustained. The absence of the Tsar from Russia encouraged a section of the Russian militia to march on Moscow, induce his half-sister Sophia to leave the monastery in which she had resided since his accession, and resume the throne. According to Voltaire, the opposition of the clergy to the sale of tobacco in Russia, which Peter had been the first Tsar to permit, was one of the principal stimuli to the revolt. The rebels had been defeated by troops loyal to Peter, before his return to Moscow, but the reprisals which he then exacted attained a severity and in some instances a refinement of cruelty for which Voltaire admits that reasons of state did not supply a sufficient excuse. In the light of recent Russian history it does, however, give one a certain chill to find him saying that instead of Peter's executing so many of his enemies it would have been more in the country's interest to put them to forced labour.

In Voltaire's eyes, and I should imagine in those of the majority of his readers, Peter's greatest achievement was the construction of St Petersburg on what was previously a marshy waste. The operation was begun in 1703 and something which Voltaire describes as a city was built in five months. It took rather longer for the Scottish and Italian architects whom Peter imported to complete the erection of one of the most beautiful cities in Europe. From the start Peter intended it to look towards Europe, in contra-distinction to Moscow, and it is an interesting fact that not only has it been restored to its former beauty, after its devastation in the last war, but its difference from Moscow has persisted. Its transformation into Leningrad has not wholly deprived it of its western orientation.

How far did Peter the Great exemplify Lord Acton's saying that absolute power corrupts absolutely? I think that he did to a very large extent. He had an unbridled temper and pursued his ends without much regard to the suffering that was caused. It is suggested by Voltaire that his second wife, who succeeded him as Catherine I, was a softening influence, to the point even where she tried to persuade him to show mercy to her stepson Alexis, in opposition to her own interests, but whatever attempt she made we have seen that it failed. Peter's attachment to her, and his belief that she would continue his policies, may rather have strengthened his resolve. The criterion by which Voltaire judged the worth of a society was the extent to which it flourished in commerce, science and the arts: a negative aspect of its advance in science was its tolerance in matters of religion. Judged in this way, the Russia of Peter the

Great comes out fairly well. There is no doubt that he developed its commerce; if he did not weaken the hold of the Orthodox Church upon the people at large, he curtailed its political power; St Petersburg became, as I have said, a most beautiful city; and while Peter's own court was hardly an ornament to the arts or sciences, it can be said to have been an indispensable precursor of the civilized court of Catherine the Great. The question, which defies an answer, like most of the unfulfilled conditionals in history, is whether the same results could not have been achieved more slowly perhaps but at a smaller human cost. The value of these results can also be put in question. The trend which Peter the Great initiated was continued by the four empresses who succeeded him, Catherine I, Anna, Elizabeth and Catherine the Great. We have seen that Voltaire was beguiled by Catherine the Great and she did indeed invite mathematicians and writers of great distinction to her court, though noticeably not Voltaire. It can, however, hardly be said that the Russia over which she ruled had yet become a civilized country.

That Voltaire would not have agreed with Acton's view of absolute power is confirmed not only by his predominantly sympathetic attitude towards Peter the Great, but by his almost unqualified enthusiasm for Louis XIV. The history of the century of Louis XIV was a book on which Voltaire worked for many years. He wrote a preface, dedicated to Lord Hervey, as early as 1740; we have noted that the book was first published in Berlin in 1752; notes were added, chiefly in reply to criticisms; and what may be regarded as the definitive edition appeared in Geneva in 1768. The reason why it was not published in France seems to have been the fear that it would elicit invidious comparisons with the current reign. Consequently, there were many pirated editions. Like all Voltaire's historical work, it is written with verve but risks being overburdened with narrative detail.

In the very first paragraph of the book Voltaire announces that it has a wider purpose than that of merely relating the life of Louis XIV. He will try to portray for posterity not just the actions of a single man, but the spirit of men in the most enlightened century that there had ever been. If it is known as the century of Louis XIV, it is because the apogee of civilization was reached in France at Louis XIV's court.

All history is much alike, he continues, for those who are interested only in committing facts to memory. But for any thinking person, or what is even rarer, any person of taste, there are only four centuries that count in the history of the world. The first, which was confined to Greece, was the century of Philip of Macedon and his son Alexander the Great, that is to say the first three quarters of the fourth century BC, though Voltaire takes it well back into the fifth century by including Pericles and Phidias among its ornaments as well as Plato, Aristotle, Demosthenes, Apelles and Praxiteles. The second was the century of Caesar and Augustus, that is the greater part of the first century BC running over into the second decade of the first century AD. Its luminaries in Voltaire's reckoning were all Roman, his list comprising Lucretius, Livy, Cicero, Virgil, Horace, Ovid, Varro and Vitruvius. The third golden age is said to be the century following the capture of Constantinople by Mahomet II in 1453. This was the period in which the arts and sciences flourished above all in Italy, especially under the patronage of the Medicis in Florence. The only names which Voltaire cites apart from the Medicis, are those of Michelangelo, Palladio and Galileo. He admits that some progress towards civilization was made during this period also in France, England, Germany and Spain but mentions only Rabelais. It is noteworthy that he allows Shakespeare to fall outside it.

Of the fourth age, the century of Louis XIV, Voltaire writes that perhaps it came closest to perfection. He takes as its starting-point the founding of the French Academy in 1635, three years before Louis XIV's birth, so that it covers two regencies, the one following his elevation to the throne in 1643, and the one following his death and the accession of his great-grandson in 1715. Voltaire writes of it that in certain respects more was accomplished in this century than in all of his other three golden ages put together.

In truth [he continues] the arts as a whole were not carried further forward than under the Medicis, Augustus and Alexander: the improvement was to be found in the development of human reason. It was the starting-point of a sound knowledge of philosophy, and one can truly say that [in the period in question] a revolution was accomplished in our arts, our minds, our manners and in our government, which should serve for ever as a sign of the true glory of our country. This happy influence was not confined to France: it extended to England and wakened the necessary spirit of rivalry in that bold and gifted nation; it brought taste to Germany and science to Russia; it reanimated Italy which had fallen into decline, and Europe owed its culture and its social sense to the court of Louis XIV.

Voltaire was not especially noted for his patriotism, but here it seems to have led him astray. If the superiority of his fourth golden age over the previous three consists above all in the progress achieved in science and philosophy, then the palm should surely go to England rather than France. Locke, Berkeley, Newton and Boyle are more than a match for Descartes, Pascal, Bayle and Montesquieu. Again, when it comes to poetry Milton, Marvell, Dryden and Pope collectively do not fall short of Racine, Corneille, Boileau and Jean-Baptiste Rousseau. Let it be granted that Molière excelled in comedy; he has no Frenchman of his own standing to back him against Congreve and the other playwrights of the English restoration. Voltaire does not mention the spread of civilization to Holland, but if Poussin and Claude were great painters, so also were Rembrandt and Vermeer. Under the heading of music in his catalogue we find only the name of Lulli. Yet the period covers the first fifty years of the life of Johann Sebastian Bach.

How then did it come about that Voltaire awarded the prize to France? It might be suggested that the reason lay partly in his self-esteem. The period which has become known in history as the Age of Enlightenment is the second half of the eighteenth century; France was its centre and it was presided over by Voltaire. Diderot and d'Holbach may have thought that he made too great a concession to deism; d'Alembert excelled him in his knowledge of mathematics and the physical sciences, but they all deferred to him. Part of the bitterness of Jean-Jacques Rousseau lay in his fury that Voltaire had been given pride of place. The theory then would be that Voltaire saw in what he called the century of Louis XIV the indispensable precursor of the Age of Enlightenment.

The main objection to this theory is one of dating. Even though Voltaire did not publish *Le Siècle de Louis Quatorze* until 1752, the letter to Lord Hervey in 1740 shows that he had already decided on its central theme: and Diderot's and d'Alembert's revised prospectus for their *Encyclopédie*, the standard-bearer of the Enlightenment, did not appear until 1750. It could be argued that Voltaire foresaw the growth of an intellectual movement with himself as its leader, and it is true that by 1740 he already saw himself as making an outstanding contribution to what Peacock was to call 'the march of mind'. Nevertheless, it is unlikely that he foresaw his own longevity or the full extent of his fame. Moreover, the Age of Enlightenment culminated in the French Revolution of which it is far from clear that Voltaire would have approved.

A simpler and more plausible hypothesis is that Voltaire was dazzled by the magnificence of Louis XIV. Indeed, he confesses as much in his letter to Lord Hervey. He admits that Louis XIV cannot claim any credit for the emergence of Newton and other great Englishmen of the period, but then he goes on to argue that Pope Leo X did not accomplish everything in the time of the Medicis. If that century is named after him, it is because he then did more for the arts than any other prince. So 'what king has rendered a greater service to humanity in this respect than Louis XIV? What king has distributed more benefactions, shown more taste and lived in such a splendid style?' He had his faults, like other men, but he was a great man with a greater reputation than any of his contemporaries. 'In spite of his depriving France of a million men, all of whom have had reason to decry him, all Europe admires him and ranks him with the greatest and the best of monarchs.'

The admission that Louis XIV cost France a million men is an allusion not, as it might superficially seem, to the civil and foreign warfare in which the country was almost constantly engaged throughout his reign, but to his revocation of the Edict of Nantes in 1685 rather less than a century after Henri IV had promulgated it. The Edict of Nantes secured toleration for the Huguenots, France's Protestant community, and its revocation sent them into exile. Many of them came to England and Voltaire goes so far as to give Louis XIV the credit for the growth of the English manufacture of silk and glass to which the Huguenots contributed. Thus Voltaire is disposed to forgive Louis even his religious bigotry which was indeed fostered in him by the most tenacious of his many mistresses, Madame de Maintenon, who not only ousted Madame de Montespan, who had borne him seven children, but after he was widowed, secretly became his wife.

It is noteworthy that all Voltaire's golden ages were periods of political turmoil. Was it because this attracted him that his first historical study was devoted to Charles XII of Sweden? At first sight, Charles XII and Louis XIV have very little in common. Even if Charles XII had not been personally engaged in warfare to the extent that we have seen, his tastes would not have led him to assemble a brilliant court. He had none of the *politesse*, the ceremonious manners, for which Voltaire so greatly admired Louis XIV. Yet the total effect of their reigns upon the fortunes of their respective countries was very similar. Louis XIV was not himself a warrior, but had able ministers in Fouquet and Colbert, a master of fortifications in Vauban, outstanding generals in Turenne, Condé and Villars. At one time France was the strongest military power in Europe. Yet the War of the Spanish Succession was disastrous for her. Had the Duchess of Marlborough not quarrelled with Queen Anne, so that Marlborough was prevented from pursuing the war, France might have ended with a smaller territory than she commanded on Louis XIV's accession. The country paid a high price for the splendours of Versailles.

At one time *Le Siècle de Louis Quatorze* formed part of a larger work in seven volumes which was published in Geneva in 1756 under the title of *Essai sur l'histoire générale et sur les moeurs et l'esprit des nations*. This universal history was the book on which we have seen that Voltaire started work in the 1730s for the edification of Madame du Châtelet. In 1769 he wrote an introduction to it for the benefit of Catherine the Great, removed the story of the century of Louis XIV, and gave it the full title, which it has since retained, of *Essai sur les moeurs et l'esprit des nations et sur les principaux faits de l'histoire depuis Charlemagne jusqu'à Louis XIII*. With the addition of Voltaire's *Annales de L'empire*, written in 1753 – a work of little interest beyond its justifying Voltaire's saying 'This agglomeration which was called, and which still calls itself the Holy Roman Empire is in no respect either holy, Roman or an empire' – the whole work occupies three vast volumes, averaging just under six hundred pages each, of the 1878 Paris edition of the complete works of Voltaire.

Voltaire's introduction is a gallop through the customs and beliefs of ancient societies. He speaks of the Chaldeans, the Indians and the Chinese as the earliest nations to be civilized. Some account is given of the progress of the Chaldeans in astronomy; the Indians are said to have been the beneficiaries of a favourable climate; their belief in reincarnation is held responsible for their pacific nature; the Chinese are said to have written reasonably as soon as they wrote at all; they were governed like a family and believed in a benevolent first principle. The earliest belief in the combination of God, the Devil, resurrection, paradise and hell is attributed to the Persians. All primitive people were subject to their priests. It was only in Greece that philosophy flourished and even there, in Voltaire's opinion, it did not amount to much.

> From Thales [he writes] until the time of Plato and Aristotle, the schools resounded with philosophical disputes, all of which revealed the wisdom and folly of the human mind, its greatness and its weakness. They nearly always argued without understanding one another, as we have done since the thirteenth century, when we began to reason. The reputation which Plato enjoyed does not surprise me; all the philosophers were unintelligible: he was as unintelligible as the rest, but he expressed himself more eloquently.

Nearly a quarter of the introduction is given over to an attack on the Old Testament. A quotation from the section on the Jews in Egypt typifies the tone of the assault:

It is to no purpose that a host of learned men find it surprising that the King of Egypt should have ordered two midwives to put to death all the male children of the Hebrews; or that the King's daughter who lived at Memphis, should have gone to bathe far from Memphis, in a branch of the Nile, where no one ever bathes because of the crocodiles. It is to no purpose that they cavil at the age of eighty which Moses had already attained before undertaking to lead a whole people out of slavery... They wonder how Pharoah could have pursued the Jews with a large body of cavalry, when all his horses had died in the fifth, sixth, seventh and tenth plagues. They wonder why six hundred thousand warriors took to flight with God in the lead, and having the advantage that all the first-born of the Egyptians had been struck dead. They again wonder why God did not give the fertile land of Egypt to his chosen people, instead of making them wander for forty years in a horrible desert.

There is only one answer to these and other countless objections, and that is: God willed it, the Church believes it and we ought to believe it.

One can sympathize with Voltaire's irony, but it is regrettable that he has allowed his resentment at the fidelity of the Christian churches to ancient Jewish myths to fester into a violent hostility towards the Jewish people. This comes out shockingly in a passage of the main volume where he contrasts the Jews with the Mahometan Arabs, to whom he attributes the same religious ferocity but much more courage and magnanimity.

In this passage Voltaire writes as if the barbarous treatment of unfriendly tribes, attributed to the Jews in the Old Testament, were still characteristic of the Jews of his own time. He upbraids them for their addiction to usury, a reproach which he was not the person to make, and one that takes no account of the fact that their exclusion from the liberal professions and the ban on their ownership of land directed their talents into the management of money. Voltaire goes so far as to call them the enemies of the human race, adding that at no time has 'that atrocious nation' been responsible for any improvement in culture, science or art. On the other hand, there was a period when the Arabs were the teachers of Europe in the sciences and the arts, even though their Koran seems inimical to the arts. What Voltaire says of the Arabs is true, but he might have given a thought to Spinoza and Maimonides.

Voltaire does not give the Jews any credit for the ten commandments, since he strongly objects to the pretence that what he calls the natural laws which are common and useful to all societies were dictated by God. These laws in Voltaire's version are: 'Thou shalt not rob or kill thy neighbour; thou shalt have a respectful care for those who gave thee life and brought thee up as a child; thou shalt not ravish thy brother's wife; thou shalt not tell lies in order to do him injury; thou shalt minister to his needs, so as to deserve to be helped in thy turn.' These 'truths' are said to be engraved on all hearts from Japan to the shores of the West. Voltaire is not so foolish as to suggest that they are universally observed. One would have to construe 'neighbour' and 'brother' very narrowly to be able to claim that they were universally acknowledged.

Apart from his effort to discredit the Old Testament, Voltaire is not concerned in his introduction with the details of ancient history. In his passing references to the Greeks and the Romans, he overlooks their polytheism, singling out Zeus and Jupiter in support of his dubious thesis that every society has believed in the existence of one supreme being. He praises both peoples for their intellectual and religious tolerance. The fate of Socrates might appear to constitute a counter-example, but Voltaire argues, I think rightly, that it had more of a political than a doctrinal ground, and anyhow that it was a crime of which the Athenians repented.

The explanation for the fall of the Roman Empire is given in a single paragraph:

The weakness of the emperors, the fractious divisions of their ministers and their eunuchs, the blood-stained quarrels nurtured in Christianity, the theological disputes displacing the exercise of arms, and lethargy displacing valour; a multitude of monks replacing farmers and soldiers; all this attracted the very barbarians who had been unable to conquer the warlike republic, but crushed a Rome languishing under emperors who were cruel, effeminate and devout.

Voltaire is consistently hostile to the fruits of the Christian religion, though he resorts to irony when attacking the religion itself.

> The amount of fraud, the errors, the disgusting stupidity in which we have been drenched for seventeen hundred years have not discredited our religion. It must be divine, since seventeen centuries of mischief and idiocy have not managed to destroy it; and we revere truth all the more for our contempt for lying.

After making easy fun of the theological absurdities of the Bishop Eusebius, an ally of Constantine's who imposed Christianity upon the Roman Empire, Voltaire amuses himself by giving a list of Constantine's major crimes, which weakened his hold upon the Romans who had never wanted him as their emperor in the first place. Voltaire suggests that it may have been for this reason, rather than the message from God which Constantine claimed to have received, that he transferred the seat of the Empire to Byzantium.

Voltaire takes less than twenty pages to cover the five centuries separating Constantine from Charlemagne who became King of the Franks in 768 AD and Holy Roman Emperor in 800. His court has been described by at least one authority as a centre of learning, though if Voltaire is to be believed, he could not sign his name. After giving a brisk account of the chief events of Charlemagne's reign, Voltaire dwells at rather greater length upon the laws and customs of the time and upon its religious beliefs. One point of interest which emerges is that a number of pious persons still believed that they would live to see the end of the world with the reappearance of Christ. I doubt, indeed, if this belief has ever been wholly extinguished, even in the twentieth century.

After leaving Charlemagne, we are taken at a fair pace through the division of his empire, the descent of the Normans into Europe and their acquisition of Naples and Sicily, the state of England before and after the Norman conquest, with a word of praise for Alfred the Great, the troubles of the papacy brought to a happy issue at the beginning of the eleventh century, with three popes dividing the revenues of the Church and each living peacefully with his mistress, the quarrels of the empire and the papacy, with the emperor Henry IV submitting to Pope Gregory VII at Canossa in 1077, the degradation of the Eastern empire, the incursion of the Moors into Spain, the exploits of Genghis Khan, the melancholy story of the Crusades, the horrible massacre of the Albigenses at the beginning of the thirteenth century. Towards the end of the first volume Voltaire delivers his verdict on the papacy:

> You will have already observed that since the death of Charlemagne we have not come across a single Roman pontiff who has not been engaged in thorny or violent disputes with emperors and kings; you will see that these quarrels continue into the century of Louis XIV, and that they are the necessary consequence of the most absurd form of government to which men have ever submitted. This absurdity consisted in letting a foreigner be master in one's own kingdom; in effect allowing him to dispense feudal rights in it, being unable to receive payment from the holders of these fiefs without his permission, and without giving him his share, being constantly liable to witness the closure at his command of temples that you have built and endowed, allowing a number of your subjects to bring lawsuits three hundred leagues away from your dominions; that is a small fraction of the chains with which the Sovereigns of Europe loaded themselves insensibly, and almost without knowing it. It is clear that if the original suggestion were made today to the council of a Sovereign, that he should submit to such practices, the person who dared to put it forward would be regarded as an utter madman. The burden, which was light at first, became gradually heavier; it was felt that it ought to be diminished, but the wisdom, knowledge and resolution were lacking to get rid of it entirely.

After touching on the relatively successful attempt of John Wycliffe in England at the end of the fourteenth century to anticipate the Reformation, and relating how John Huss, his counterpart in Bohemia, was lured to his martyrdom, Voltaire proceeds to give a succinct review of the Hundred Years War. He gives Joan of Arc due credit for restoring the fortunes of France, reserving his sarcasms for his poem *La Pucelle*. There follows a chapter of ten pages on the state of the sciences and arts in the thirteenth and fourteenth centuries. Italy and especially Florence was then the

centre of European culture and Voltaire mentions the painters Cima-
bue and Giotto, the architect Brunelleschi, and the poets Dante,
Petrarch and Boccaccio. Consistently with his view that literature
progresses, he remarks that these writers have been surpassed by
Ariosto and Tasso in the fifteenth and sixteenth centuries. It is
characteristic of him also that he devotes several paragraphs to the
popular belief that the ass on which Jesus rode into Jerusalem walked
over the waters to Verona, and its exploitation by Pope Boniface
VIII who drew the profitable inference that if the ass was capable
of such mobility the Virgin Mary's house could have made its way
to Loreto, where the house was transformed into a handsome
church. Nor could Voltaire refrain from a gibe at scholasticism.

> If [he writes] the light shone only on Tuscany, it wasn't as if there
> was no talent anywhere else. St Bernard and Abélard in France,
> in the twelfth century, can be regarded as men of superior intellect;
> but their tongue was a barbarous jargon, and they paid tribute in
> Latin to the bad taste of their time. The rhyme to which those Latin
> hymns of the twelfth and thirteenth centuries was subjected set the
> seal on barbarity. That was not how Horace wrote his secular songs.
> Scholastic theology, the bastard daughter of Aristotle's philosophy,
> badly translated and misunderstood, did more harm to reason and
> scholarship than the Huns and the Vandals had done.

Proceeding on his rapid way, noting the conquests of Tamerlane,
the fall of Constantinople, the wickedness of King Louis XI of
France, the Wars of the Roses in England and the decline of feudalism, Voltaire congratulates Ferdinand and Isabella of Spain not
only on their success in defeating the Moors at the end of the fifteenth
century but also on their expulsion of the Jews, against whom he
delivers yet another virulent tirade, despite his surprising aside that
'at bottom we are no more than Jews with a foreskin'. After giving
a passing salute to Galileo and his predecessor Copernicus, who
first caused the light of 'true philosophy' to shine upon men in
the sixteenth century, in spite of the efforts of the Church to put
it out, Voltaire concentrates upon the chequered career of the Holy
Roman Emperor Charles V, who abdicated in 1556 having had to

defend his possessions both against Sulaiman II the Magnificent, Sultan of the Ottoman Empire, and against Francis I, one of the more powerful of the Kings of France. Another of Charles's serious problems lay in the political consequences of the Reformation to which Voltaire devotes ten chapters, followed by one on the state of religion in France under Francis I and his successors, one on the religious orders, and one on the Inquisition. In those first ten chapters, Luther is given pride of place, with Calvin a close second, and mention is also made of the violent Anabaptists, of Zwingli, a Swiss who denied the Eucharistic presence, of Servetus, a Spanish theologian who went too far and was condemned by Calvin to be burned at the stake for denying the Trinity and the divinity of Christ, of the establishment of the Anglican Church under Henry VIII, and of the triumph of Calvinism in Scotland. Voltaire sums up the religious issue in a couple of sentences: 'So, while those who were called Papists ate God but not bread, the Lutherans ate both bread and God. Soon after there came the Calvinists who ate bread and did not eat God.' Not one to overlook the state of corruption into which the Roman Catholic Church had fallen, he also makes the obvious point that the questions at issue were not merely theological.

Going back a little in time, Voltaire turns his attention to the exploits of the Spaniards and the Portuguese at the end of the fourteenth and the beginning of the fifteenth centuries, notably the discovery of Japan and Abyssinia, the circumnavigation of the globe, the discovery of America, the conquest of Mexico and Peru. Voltaire finds it problematic whether Europe has profited by its incursion into America.

It is certain that at the outset the Spaniards drew great riches from it; but Spain was depopulated and the fact that the treasures were shared at the end by so many other nations restored the equality which they had at first upset. The price of commodities has everywhere increased. So no one has really gained. It remains to be seen whether cochineal and quinine are sufficiently valuable to make up for the loss of so many men.

The French retained relatively few possessions in the New World: Martinique, Guadeloupe, some small islands in the Antilles and half the island of San Domingo, for which they were indebted to their pirates. Voltaire reckoned that in the French part of San Domingo in 1757 there was a free population of 30,000 living off the labour of 100,000 black and mulatto slaves, and this gave him the opportunity for an eloquent denunciation of slavery.

> We tell them that they are men like ourselves, that they are redeemed by the blood of a God who died for their sake, and then they are made to work like beasts of burden; they are worse fed; if they try to escape they have a leg cut off; they are given a wooden leg and put to the manual labour of turning the shaft of a sugar mill. And then we have the effrontery to talk about human rights.

After giving an account of the revenues which France derived from the colonies, Voltaire concludes 'This commerce does not enrich a country; quite the contrary, it destroys men, it causes shipwrecks; it is questionable whether it is a real good; but since men have created new needs, it saves France from having to buy dearly abroad a luxury which has become a necessity.' In appraising Voltaire, we should remember that the very first onslaught on the institution of slavery in the New World, the British abolition of the slave trade, did not take place until nearly thirty years after his death.

The sixteenth century to which Voltaire's narrative returns saw the rise of England and Holland at the expense of Spain and the death of Francis. He expresses some admiration for Queen Elizabeth while deploring her treatment of Mary Queen of Scots. His account of the misfortunes of France overlaps with his poem *La Henriade*. He duly denounces the massacre of Saint Bartholemew's day on 24 August 1572, on which several thousand Huguenots were murdered, linking it with the Counter-Reformation, endorsed in 1563 by the Council of Trent, which had taken twenty-one years to agree on the anathemas that it finally pronounced. The Council helped to foment the religious wars of the following century.

Since Voltaire is purporting to write a history of the world he intersperses his European narrative with chapters, usually short, on India, Persia, the Ottoman Empire, the African coast, Morocco, and the Far East. A whole chapter is devoted to the battle of Lepanto in 1571 when a Christian fleet gathered together by Pope Pius V, Philip II King of Spain and the rulers of Venice and commanded by Don Juan of Austria, bastard son of Charles V, defeated the Turks. This battle earned Don Juan a place in history but as Voltaire does not fail to point out, its consequences were nugatory. Venice gained no territory by it and the Turks retook Tunis in 1574.

In writing about Asians, Africans, and Orientals, Voltaire tends to exaggerate the differences between them and Europeans. The following passage is typical:

> The difference between Eastern customs and our own, as great as the difference between our languages, is a subject fit for the attention of a philosopher. The most civilized peoples of these vast countries have nothing in common with our civilization; their arts are not ours. Food, clothing, houses, gardens, laws, worship, manners, all are different. Is there anything more contrary to our customs than the way in which merchants bargain in Hindustan? The most important deals are concluded, without speech or writing; everything is done by signs. How could there not be such numerous differences between oriental customs and our own? Nature is fundamentally the same everywhere, but the differences between their climate and ours are enormous. In southern India puberty is reached at the age of seven or eight. Marriages are often contracted there at that age. Those children, who become fathers, enjoy a measure of reason which nature grants them at an age when our reason is scarcely developed.
>
> All these peoples resemble us only in their passions, and in the universal reason which offsets the passions, and imprints on human hearts the law. 'Do not do to others what you would not want to have done to you.' These are the two characteristics which nature stamps on so many different human races, and the two external bonds by which she unites them, in spite of everything that divides them. All the rest is the fruit of the sun, the earth and custom.

In general Voltaire likes to find a salient characteristic or set of characteristics in the people whom he describes, such as the morality of the Chinese, the military skill of the Tartars, the addiction of the Persians to astrology and their excellence in poetry. He finds next to nothing to admire in the character of the American Indians, saying of the Peruvians, who worshipped the sun, that they alone of all the American people had a religion which was not obviously irrational. He then goes on to condemn the Mexican indulgence in human sacrifice. It is to Voltaire's credit that he devotes a chapter to the extraordinary achievements of the Jesuit missionaries in Paraguay who gradually gained control of the country at the beginning of the seventeenth century and ruled it until the middle of the eighteenth, when, at the instigation of the papacy, they were ousted by the Portuguese, operating from Brazil. So far from exploiting the Indians, they brought them prosperity, instructed them in agriculture, industry, architecture and military self-defence. They governed them justly and gave them the benefits of communism, without its perversions, employing gold and silver to embellish their churches but not to enrich themselves. It is perhaps the only place and time where the introduction of Christianity has been wholly beneficial, barring the fact that the Paraguayan Indians were not entrusted with self-government.

After a long chapter on the achievements of Cardinal Richelieu, a brief review of the state of Spain in the seventeenth century, where Voltaire, without mentioning Velasquez, is able to discover only a few painters of the second rank, and a slightly longer account of the misfortunes of the Empire and the suffering of Germany in the Thirty Years War, Voltaire devotes four chapters to the history of England. Conventionally, he condemns the Gunpowder Plot, pities Charles I, respects Cromwell and applauds the 'theism' of the court of Charles II and the foundation of the Royal Society. There follows a review of the state of Italy, with some praise for Pope Gregory XII and his introduction of the Gregorian calendar, and for his successor Pope Sixtus V, who reformed the papal administration, enriched the Vatican library and carried out Michelangelo's design for the dome of St Peter's. We are then treated to a series of chapters in which the fortunes of Holland, Sweden, Denmark, Poland and Russia are swiftly recalled. The principal events, in the record, are the revolt against Spain of the seven provinces of Holland, under the Princes of Orange, and the exploits of the Dutch Navy, the substitution in Denmark in 1660 of an absolute for an elective monarchy, the conquests of Gustavus Adolphus of Sweden, the defeat of the Turks outside Vienna in 1683 by an army commanded by John Sobieski, King of Poland, and the usurpation of the throne of Russia by Boris Godunov, who reigned from 1598 to 1605. A parade of the rulers of the Ottoman Empire, beginning with Mahomet III, who is said to have inaugurated his reign by causing nineteen of his brothers to be strangled and twelve of his father's pregnant widows to be drowned, is followed in rapid order by an account of civil strife in Persia exacerbated by religious differences, a résumé of the career of the Mogul emperor Aurangzeb, the story of the establishment of the Manchu dynasty in China, and that of the expulsion of all foreigners, including Christian missionaries, from Japan.

Voltaire concludes his work with a short retrospective commentary. Towards the end he deplores the cost to European civilization of the entombment in monasteries of an astonishing number of useless men and women. He also considers it regrettable that Europe should have been in such a constant state of warfare, often for very slender reasons. A contemporary reader may find it ironical that Voltaire feels entitled to remark that the conduct of war has grown more humane and that the cities which are fought over change their ownership without much disturbance to the civilians who inhabit them. I quote his final paragraphs:

> There were long periods when Germany, France and England were afflicted by civil wars; but the damage was soon repaired and the flourishing state of these countries shows that human industry has by far prevailed over human fury. Things are not the same in Persia, for instance, which has been a prey to devastation for forty years; but if it is united under a wise prince, it will recover its solidity in less time than it lost it.
>
> When a nation is mistress of the arts, when it is not subjugated and deformed by foreigners, it rises easily from its ruins, and always regains its health.

Lytton Strachey in the chapter on Hume included in the section 'Six English Historians' of his *Portraits in Miniature* writes of Voltaire, who outlived Hume by nearly two years though he was born over sixteen years earlier, that he 'was indeed a master of narrative, but was usually too much occupied with discrediting Christianity to be a satisfactory historian.' If sufficient emphasis is laid on Voltaire's mastery of narrative, I think that this verdict is just.

5

The *Philosophical Dictionary*

In its original form, Voltaire's *Dictionnaire philosophique portatif* (Pocket Philosophical Dictionary) was nearly as much of a misnomer as 'The Holy Roman Empire'. Very few of the 118 essays of which it consisted were philosophical in the current sense of the term and their only claim to forming a dictionary was that they were presented in alphabetical order. Voltaire first had the idea of composing a 'pocket dictionary' of this type when he was living in Berlin in 1752, but did not publish it until 1764, when it was printed in London. Since it was predominantly an attack on the theories and practices of the several forms of Christianity, showing little respect for the New Testament and none whatsoever for the Old, it was considered outrageously subversive, to the point where Voltaire found it prudent to disavow its authorship. Typically, he also proceeded to expand it, so that when he reissued it in 1770 he ceased to characterize it as a 'pocket' dictionary. Later editors combined this 'philosophical' work with Voltaire's contributions to Diderot's and d'Alembert's encyclopedia, which were not very numerous or important, with his more interesting *Questions sur l'Encyclopédie*, which also dates from 1770, and with a number of his miscellaneous writings, the whole still arranged in alphabetical order, and by now even containing a few definitions. The result was that in the 1878–9 Paris edition of Voltaire's complete works the section entitled 'Dictionnaire philosophique' ran to four large volumes, comprising well over 600 entries and amounting in all to nearly 2,500 pages. It is this work that I now propose to examine.

While the anti-religious note is still dominant, the area over which the material ranges has grown very wide. In addition to ecclesiastical history and criticism, it covers physics, biology, etymology, anthropology, medicine, law, politics and morals; there are frequent incursions into literature and a number of short biographies. Only the arts are neglected, in as much as there is scarcely any reference to architecture, sculpture, painting or music. On the other hand, we shall see that the absence of what we now count as philosophy from the original *Philosophical Dictionary* has been made good to quite a considerable extent.

I intend to discuss Voltaire's religious views, both because of their historical importance and still more because of the part that they played in his general attitude to life. At the same time I do not think it necessary to reiterate his criticisms either of the characters who figure in the Old Testament or of the behaviour which is attributed to them. I hope that by now it can be taken for granted that the accounts of creation and the origin of man which appear in the Book of Genesis are not only inconsistent but independently ridiculous, that the whole of the Pentateuch is riddled with absurdities, and that the best that can be said for the remainder of the Canon is that much of it, like the Song of Solomon and the Book of Ecclesiastes, is outstanding for its literary merit. Voltaire repeatedly professes to be shocked by the wickedness of David and other Jewish leaders and by the savagery which the Jews displayed towards other nations, at the reported bidding of their tribal deity. No doubt this is the principal reason for his expressions of anti-Semitism, but as we have already noted they go well beyond it. Denunciations of the Jews occur as frequently in his *Dictionnaire philosophique* as they do in his historical writings. This is curiously at variance with Voltaire's general tendency to champion the cause of the oppressed. The only concession that he makes in this instance is a refusal to endorse the practice of the Inquisition. He asserts that however vile the Jews may be, they should not be burned at the stake for their religious beliefs.

Voltaire was not himself an atheist but a deist. He thought that he had rational grounds for the belief that there is a necessary eternal supreme intelligent being, by whom the universe is governed. He did not consider it demonstrable that there is such a being, but he thought it vastly more probable than the alternative hypothesis that the order which is discernible in the world and the intelligence and sensitivity which are exhibited not only by human beings but also by many species of animals, are the product of an ultimately fortuitous collection of material atoms. In short, he accepted what is most commonly known as the argument from design.

This argument was effectively answered in two works appearing shortly after Voltaire's death, David Hume's *Dialogues Concerning Natural Religion*, posthumously published in 1779, and Immanuel Kant's *Critique of Pure Reason*, the first edition of which was published in 1781. Kant termed it the physico-theological argument and rejected it on the ground that it presupposed the fallacious ontological argument, in which a vain attempt is made to represent the mere concept of God as entailing his existence. This view of the argument from design originated with Kant and the strongest objections which Voltaire considered that he had to meet were those set out in Baron d'Holbach's *Système de la nature*, which was published in 1770. In his entry on 'Final Causes' Voltaire quotes an 'elegant and dangerous passage' of this book at length:

It is claimed that animals provide us with convincing evidence of a powerful cause of their existence; we are told that the wonderful agreement of their parts, observed in their reciprocally aiding one another to fulfil their functions and maintain their unity, points to the existence of a workman who combines power with wisdom. We cannot doubt the power of nature; she produces all the animals that we observe, by means of combinations of matter which is continuously active; the adjustment of the parts of these animals is a consequence of the necessary laws of their nature and their combination: as soon as this adjustment ceases, the animal necessarily perishes. What then becomes of the wisdom, the intelligence or the goodness of the alleged cause which was credited with this vaunted adjustment? Where do we find the wisdom, the goodness, the fore-sight, the immutability of a workman who appears to be solely concerned with disarranging and breaking the springs of the machines which are presented as the masterpieces of his power and skill? If this God cannot act otherwise, he is neither free nor all-powerful. If he is infirm of purpose, he is not immutable. If he allows the machines which he has endowed with sensitivity to suffer pain, he is lacking in goodness. If he has not managed to make his products stronger, he is lacking in skill. When we observe that animals perish, like all the other works of the Divinity, we cannot avoid concluding either that all the activity of nature is necessary and no more than the consequence of natural laws, or that the workman who devised this activity is devoid alike of purpose, power, constancy, skill and goodness.

There follow two paragraphs in the first of which the misfortunes of men are cited as evidence that they are not favoured by a God and in the second of which it is argued that nature is not an artefact, since the explanation for all its workings can be found within it. The passage then proceeds:

But let us suppose for a moment that it is impossible to conceive of the universe without a workman who created it and watches over his creation, where are we to situate this workman? Is he to be inside or outside the universe? Is he matter or movement? Or is he merely space, nullity, the void? In any case, either he would be a nonentity, or he would be contained in nature and subject to its laws. If he is within nature, all that I can observe there is matter in movement, and I must conclude that the agent who sets it in motion is corporeal and material and consequently liable to perish. If this agent is outside nature, I then lack any idea of the place which he occupies, or of an immaterial being, or of the way in which an unextended spirit can act upon matter with which it has no connection. Those unknown spaces, which the imagination situates beyond the visible world, do not exist for a being which hardly sees further than its feet; the only way in which I can conceive of the ideal power which inhabits them is by fantasizing some random combination of the colours which my imagination cannot discover elsewhere than in the world where I am; in that case I shall merely be reproducing ideally what my senses will have perceived in fact; and this God, whom I endeavour to distinguish from nature and put beyond its grasp, will always be bound to return within it, whether I like it or not.

It will still be objected that if a statue or a watch were shown to a savage who had never seen such things, he could not help acknowledging that they were the work of some intelligent agent, more skilful and more creative than himself: from this it is to be inferred that we are equally forced to acknowledge that the machine of the universe, man, the phenomena of nature, are the works of an agent whose intelligence and power far excels our own.

I reply, first of all, that we cannot doubt that nature is very powerful and creative; we admire its creativity every time that we are struck by the far-reaching, varied and complicated effects that we discover in those of its works on which we take the trouble to reflect: even so it is neither more nor less creative in any one of its works than in the others. We understand no better how it can produce a stone or a metal than a brain like Newton's. We call a man creative when he can do things that we cannot do ourselves. Nature can do everything; and the mere fact that something exists is a proof that nature has the power to bring it about. It is we ourselves who supply the standard by reference to which we judge nature to be creative; we compare nature to ourselves, and as we possess a quality which we call intelligence by means of which we produce works displaying our creativity, we infer that the works of nature do not belong to it, but are due to a workman with an intelligence like our own – but one that we apportion to the wonder that his works arouse in us, that is to say to our weakness and our ignorance.

Voltaire replies to this argument both in the course of the entry on Final Causes in which he quotes it and in a section of his entry on God and Gods. His principal point is that d'Holbach does no more than deify nature. In default of any detailed account of the way in which material atoms combine to produce natural phenomena, including the manifestations of human intelligence and sensibility, the attribution to nature of a creative power, to whose mysterious activity everything is finally referred, is tantamount to the acknowledgement of an unknown deity.

There is some force in this contention. Certainly the case for materialism has been very much strengthened by the development of the theory of evolution and still more by the progress achieved in the sciences of physiology and biochemistry. It should, however, also be noted that Voltaire fails to dispose of d'Holbach's point about the situation of the deity. If he is placed outside time, then not only does it come into question whether such a being is conceivable but, as Kant argued, the concept of causality does not extend to him. If he is placed within time, nature absorbs him. I am not sure what to make of the concept of an original event, but even if it can be intelligibly satisfied, there is no reason why the event that satisfies it should be in any way personified, still less made a fitting object for any act of worship.

Voltaire sometimes writes as if all that is needed to establish his case is the acknowledgement of the prevalence in nature of what Hume called 'the curious adapting of means to ends' with its resemblance to 'the productions of human contrivance', but if this was his opinion, he failed to see the force of the objection which is implicit in d'Holbach's argument, though more clearly stated by Hume, that nature cannot fail to exhibit some sort of order and that there is no reason a priori why the regularities which we discover in it should not be captured by teleological as well as mechanical formulae. What Voltaire needed to show at the very least was that some purpose is discernible in the universe as a whole. I see no reason to suppose that this requirement can be satisfied, and the only ground on which Voltaire attempts to meet it is patently fallacious. He advances his argument in the course of a brief dismissal of the philosophy of Spinoza, whose identification of God with Nature might well have attracted him had he not seen it as making too dangerous a concession to d'Holbach. He attacks Spinoza for being obscure, for writing bad Latin, and, more seriously, for being inconsistent and for denying final causes. So far as I can make it out, it is in the denial of final causes that the inconsistency is supposed to lie. For Spinoza, reality is a single substance, of which one attribution is extension and another is thought.

If [says Voltaire] this universal infinite being thinks, how should it fail to have purposes? If it has purposes, how should it fail to have a will? According to Spinoza, we are modes of this absolute, necessary, infinite being. I say to Spinoza: We have wills, we make plans, we who are only modes: therefore this infinite, necessary, absolute being cannot lack them: therefore it has will, purposes, power.

Spinoza's philosophy is, indeed, difficult to understand, but it would seem to have been his view that the intelligence, purpose and power which is attributable to the single substance is articulated in the various modes of its infinite attributes. He would have thought it nonsensical to ascribe such properties to the substance, independently of its attributes and their diversification, which is what Voltaire's argument requires. Neither would there be any warrant for such an ascription even if Spinoza had succeeded, as it seems to me obvious that he does not, in making out the world to be a logical unity.

Another source of Voltaire's annoyance with Spinoza was that Spinoza followed Descartes in identifying matter with extension. Not only did Voltaire believe that these philosophers were thereby disqualified from admitting the possibility of motion, but for some reason which I do not understand he allied his deism to the Newtonian view that portions of matter were separated by empty space. It looks at one point as if he thought that the conception of God as an infinite being, whatever that might mean, was consistent with allowing space to be infinite but not with allowing matter to be so. What is curious is that he raises this issue only in connection with the occupation of space, denying, for instance, that matter is infinitely divisible, but refusing either to affirm or deny that it exists infinitely in time. Oddly enough he accepts the ancient principle *ex nihilo nihil fit*, that is, that there can be no creation out of nothing, but takes it to imply no more than that if anything exists at any time something must have existed eternally, as though God might have spun matter out of himself. In his entry on God and Gods he asserts confidently that his reason convinces him that there must be an eternal being who imposes its order on matter, but not that matter must have been created by it. He allows the possibility that matter is independently necessary and eternal. This leads him to wonder why, if we are going to commit ourselves to the existence of more than one necessary being, we should stop at two: why not go so far as thirty? Presumably, this is meant to suggest that we should try to manage with one, though rather than venture on this enterprise Voltaire subsides into talk of the weakness of our understanding. In his entry on Infinity he shows himself unable to conceive of time itself as other than infinite but makes no attempt to relate it to the concept of his deity.

Voltaire's hazardous argument that God must possess the properties with which he has endowed his creatures induces him to credit his deity not only with intelligence but also with a situation in space, from which it should follow that he is corporeal, a conclusion which Voltaire does not positively endorse but recognizes as a commonplace of ancient thought. He avoids discussing the question how much space God momentarily or eternally occupies. Neither does he endow him with every human, let alone animal or purely physical disposition, which would indeed make his existence logically impossible unless some of the dispositions were merely latent; and then it would seem to be arbitrary which ones were actualized. Voltaire would have liked to be able to represent his deity as benevolent and in the course of his entry on Aristotle, a philosopher whom he chooses to admire, as opposed to Plato, whom he consistently denigrates, he assumes that God has implanted in every heart the knowledge of goodness together with some inclination towards evil. One might expect Voltaire to argue that God did this for some reason, but instead he surprises his readers by taking the line that God could not have chosen otherwise. He maintains not only that both God and matter necessarily exist and that this necessity extends to God's ordering of the world, but that everything that happens would still be necessary, even if there had been no God to preside over nature. I quote a decisive passage from his entry on Fate (*Destin*):

Either the world subsists on its own, by means of its physical laws, or a supreme being has fashioned it in accordance with his supreme laws: in either case, these laws are immutable; in either case everything is necessary; heavy bodies are disposed to gravitate towards the centre of the earth; they can have no disposition to rest in the air. Pear trees cannot yield pineapples. A spaniel's instinct cannot be that of an ostrich; everything is ordered, geared and limited.

A man can have only a certain number of teeth, of hairs and of ideas; there comes a time when he necessarily loses his teeth, his hair and his ideas.

It is a contradictory proposition that what happened yesterday may not have happened, that what is happening today may not be; it is also a contradictory proposition that what is bound to be might not be so bound.

If you could alter the fate of a fly, there would be no reason to prevent your determining the fate of all the other flies, of all other animals, of all men, of all nature; eventually you would find yourself more powerful than God.

After dismissing 'fools' who produce examples to show that doctors and politicians influence the course of events, and peasants who think that hail fell by chance on their fields, whereas philosophers know that there is no such thing as chance, Voltaire continues:

There are people whose fear of this truth leads them to grant half of it, like debtors who offer half to their creditors, and ask to be let off the rest. Some events are necessary, they say, and others not. It would be ridiculous if one part of the world were ordered, and the other not; if part of what happens had to happen, and another part of what happens did not have to. When one takes a closer view, one sees that the denial of fatalism is absurd; but there are many people fated to reason otherwise; others fated not to reason at all; others to persecute those who do reason.

Some people tell you: Don't believe in fatalism, for then, since everything will seem to you inevitable, you won't work at anything, you will sink into indifference. You won't care for wealth, or honour or praise; you won't want to obtain anything, you won't think of yourself as having any merit or power; no talent will be cultivated, everything will be lost in apathy.

Don't be afraid, gentlemen, we shall always have passions and prejudices, since it is our fate to be subject to prejudices and passions; we shall realize that it no more depends on us that we have high deserts and great talent than that we have a good head of hair and a well-turned hand; we shall be convinced that we should not be vain about anything, and yet we shall always be vain.

I am necessarily impelled to write this; and you, you are impelled to condemn me: we are both of us equally stupid, equally the playthings of fate. It is your nature to do evil; mine is to love truth and to publish it in spite of you.

Voltaire's reasoning in this passage is not impeccable. He does not sufficiently distinguish the harmless tautology that everything is what it is, has been what it has been, and will be what it will be, from the debatable proposition that nothing could ever be otherwise, or in other words that every event is causally determined. Voltaire makes no attempt to prove this proposition, being content to assert that what we call chance is not and cannot be anything other than the unknown cause of a known effect. This was a more plausible assertion in Voltaire's day than it would be now, when it is believed by most scientific experts that the fundamental laws of physics are statistical. If they are right, it still remains possible that macroscopic events, including all human behaviour, are amenable to strictly causal generalizations. In my view this is not a matter which can be settled a priori. To uphold determinism at this level is, as it were, to wager that the relevant causal theories will be empirically established; and this remains an open question.

One way of closing it would be to vindicate a concept of free will which entails indeterminism, but I have to say that I do not believe this to be feasible. Neither, obviously, did Voltaire. Here, as elsewhere in philosophy, his mentor is John Locke. They both hold that a man is free to the extent that he has the power to act as he chooses. In Locke's words: 'So far as a man has power to think or not to think, to move or not to move, according to the preference or direction of his own mind, so far is a man *free*.'[1]

[1] *Essay Concerning Human Understanding*, II.xxi.8.

English influence John Locke

On the other hand, neither Locke nor Voltaire is disposed to attach any sense to the question whether our wills are free. To quote Locke again: 'Liberty, which is but a power, belongs only to *agents*, and cannot be an attribute or a modification of the will which is also but a power.'[1] To which he adds a little later on: 'Powers are relations not agents: and that which has the power or not the power to operate, is that alone which is or is not free, and not the power itself. For freedom, or not freedom, can belong to nothing, but what has or has not a power to act.'[2]

I own that, unlike Voltaire, I am not entirely convinced by Locke's reasoning here. I think that I can discern sense not only in the question, which Locke allows, whether on a given occasion a person is able to give effect to his choices but also to the question, which he disallows, whether he could have chosen otherwise than as he did. The problem is to give an acceptable analysis of this second question. I once subscribed to an analysis which allowed it to be true both that a person could have chosen otherwise, and that his choice was causally determined, but I have since come to doubt whether this was correct. I shall not pursue this question here, since it would be of no comfort to the moralist to have choices escape the net of causality only to fall into the embrace of chance. I know that reliance is sometimes placed on an alleged distinction between reasons and causes, but even if this distinction holds good, which I disbelieve, it fails the libertarian, since his antagonist can then raise the question how it comes about that the person acts for the effective reason rather than some other.

Notoriously, as we shall see when we come to describe Voltaire's most famous work *Candide*, he did not consider that this is the best of all possible worlds. Together with his acceptance of determinism, this puts a strain upon his deism. In a section of his entry on Final Causes he comes near to joining the company of those whom we have seen him mocking as half-way necessitarians. 'It follows,' he says, 'from the nature of things, that a particular man

[1] Ibid., xiv.
[2] Ibid., xix.

should be ambitious, that this man should sometimes raise an army of other men, that he should be victorious or defeated; but one will never be entitled to say: Man has been created by God in order to be killed in a war.'

Why not? Merely, it would appear, because not every man is so killed; there are other ways of dying. But all that this shows is that the hypothesis of final causes operates only at a very general level. It does not handle every particular event. Voltaire still has to admit that a man's death in battle, even if not explicitly designed by his creator, is still the inexorable effect of the natural order which the creator has designed.

So the dilemma remains. Either the deity is not wholly benevolent or he is not omniscient or not all-powerful. Voltaire has the honesty to confront it and makes an unusual choice. He concedes that his deity is neither omniscient nor all-powerful. This emerges in a series of propositions in his entry on Power, which are sufficiently remarkable to be quoted in full. They are all the more interesting in that they occur in the context of an attempted rebuttal of the Manichean doctrine, attributed also to Zoroaster, that the world is a field of conflict between good and evil powers.

> You are [writes Voltaire] forced to admit an intelligence spread over the universe, but
> 1. Do you know, for example, if this power extends so far as to predict the future? You have asserted that it does a thousand times; but you have never been able to prove it or to understand it. You cannot know how a being of any kind sees what is not. Well, the future is not: so no being can see it. You are reduced to saying that he foresees it; but foreseeing is a matter of conjecture.

I interrupt Voltaire at this point to remark that his reasoning here has gone astray. The future is not, only in the sense that it is not yet, just as the past is not, in the sense that it is no longer. Logically, the fact that the future is yet to come no more entails that it cannot be foreseen than the fact that the past has ceased to be entails that it cannot be remembered. If we can make sense of there being a deity at all, we should not be logically forbidden to think of him as being omniscient without being omnipotent, or indeed the converse. He might have planned the universe and chosen to forget all about it. I do not know that either of these opinions has ever been seriously held. The Epicureans came nearest to the second of them with their belief that the gods took no interest in the world at all. But now I am digressing. The sting of Voltaire's first proposition lies in its second paragraph:

> Well, a God who, in your view, makes conjectures can be mistaken. He really has made a mistake in your system; for if he had foreseen that his enemy would poison all his works here below, he would not have produced them; he would not have himself invited the shame of being continually defeated.

2. Do I not do him much more honour in saying that all his actions proceed from the necessity of his nature than you do in supplying him with an enemy who deforms, sullies, destroys all his works here below?

3. One's idea of God is not unworthy of him if one says that, having created thousands of worlds in which there was neither death nor evil, he was bound to admit evil and death into this one.

4. It is not lowering to God to say that he could not create man without giving him self-love; that this self-love could not guide a man without nearly always leading him astray; that man's passions are necessary but harmful; that propagation cannot be carried on without desires; that desires cannot move men to action without quarrels; that the quarrels necessarily lead to wars, etc.

There follow two paragraphs in the first of which it is asserted, surprisingly, that it would be foolish to credit nature with the power of preventing tempests, plagues and other physical scourges, and in the second that while it needed a powerful being to create lions who devoured bulls and men who invented arms to kill not only bulls and lions but one another, such a being was not required to be all powerful. Then:

7. If the great Being had been infinitely powerful, there is no reason why he should not have made sensitive animals infinitely happy; he did not do so, therefore he could not.

8. All philosophical sects have foundered on the reef of physical and moral evil. One is reduced to admitting that God having done his best, could not do better.

9. This necessity settles all the difficulties and puts an end to all the disputes. We have not the effrontery to say: Everything is well; we say: Everything goes as little badly as it could.

10. Why does a child often die at its mother's breast? Why does another have the misfortune to be born to a life of torment and a dreadful death?

There follows a catalogue of the evils that flesh is heir to, ending with the comment 'Twist and turn as you will, you will find no other solution than that everything has been necessary.'

All this comes perilously close to the admission that this is after all the best of all possible worlds. I disregard the suggestion, as unintelligible, that this was fated to be the one exception to all the blissful worlds that God has also created. The view which I think that we should attribute to Voltaire is that this is not the best possible world in as much as any number of better worlds are imaginable, but that it is the best possible in the sense that God lacked the power to improve it. God is acquitted of malevolence by being cast into the toils of necessity. Voltaire fails to see that this makes his deity superfluous. I do not think that he is being ironical in ascribing so much weakness to him. He becomes ironical only at the end of the essay when he says that the way out of the labyrinth is to be found in faith.

To see that this is so we need only consult the second section of his entry on Faith.

Divine faith [he asserts] about which so much has been written is evidently nothing but a suppression of disbelief; for certainly the only faculty we have which can give rise to belief is the understanding, and the objects of faith are not objects of the understanding. One can believe only what seems true; and nothing can seem true except in one of three ways, either by intuition, sensation: *I exist, I see the sun*; or by an accumulation of probabilities which do duty for certainty: *there is a town called Constantinople*; or by way of demonstration: *triangles which have the same base and apex are equal*.

Faith, having nothing to do with any of that, can no more be a belief, a conviction, than it can be yellow or red. It can therefore only be an abolition of reason, a silence of worship in the face of incomprehensible things. So, to speak philosophically, no one believes in the Trinity, no one believes that the same body can be in a thousand places at once; and he who says: I believe in these mysteries, if he reflects on his thought, will see, without any possibility of doubt, that what these words mean is: I respect these mysteries; I submit to those who proclaim them to me; for they agree with me that neither my reason nor theirs believes in them; well, it is clear that when my reason is not convinced, I am not: my reason and I cannot be two different beings. It is absolutely contradictory that I should find true what my understanding finds false. Faith is therefore only a suppression of disbelief.

Voltaire is right to the extent that if one thinks that one has good reason to believe a proposition, one cannot simultaneously hold it to be false. It does not follow, however, that one cannot hold irrational beliefs or even beliefs that are self-contradictory, or absurd, without perceiving that they are so. There is nothing psychologically impossible about the claim of the White Queen in *Alice Through the Looking Glass* to have succeeded in believing 'six impossible things before breakfast'. Voltaire should have been content to argue that an appeal to faith is not a justification for a belief and, more importantly, that it does not serve to turn nonsense into sense.

Though it adds nothing to the argument, an excerpt from the next section, which is the first of the sections on Faith in the original Pocket Dictionary, is worth including for its greater fidelity to Voltaire's usual style. Pico della Mirandola and the Borgia Pope, Alexander VI, are represented as discussing the paternity of the child which the Pope's daughter Lucrezia is carrying. Both believe her husband to be impotent but Pico still professes faith in the husband's being the father. When Alexander asks him how he can be so silly, Pico replies that he accepts greater absurdities on faith such as 'that a serpent talked, that since then all men were damned and that Balaam's ass was also very eloquent'. He continues his recital of absurdities until Alexander collapses into laughter.

'I believe all that as you do,' he said, 'for I am well aware that I can be saved only by faith, and that I shall not be saved by my works.' 'Ah! Holy Father,' said Pico, 'You don't need either works or faith: that is good for poor laymen like us; but you who are the vicar of God, you can believe and do what you like. You have the keys of heaven, and doubtless Saint Peter will not shut the door in your face. But as for me, I confess that I should need more powerful protection, if, being only a poor prince, I had slept with my daughter and if I had employed the stiletto and poison as often as your Holiness.' Alexander could take a joke. 'Let us speak seriously,' he said to Prince della Mirandola. 'Tell me what is the virtue of telling God that one is convinced of things of which in fact one cannot be convinced. What pleasure can that give God? Between ourselves, to say that one believes what it is impossible to believe is to lie.' Pico della Mirandola made a big sign of the Cross. 'Ah! God the Father,' he exclaimed, 'may your Holiness forgive me, you are not a Christian.' 'No, i'faith,' said the Pope. 'I suspected that you were not,' said Pico della Mirandola.

Voltaire's acceptance of determinism may make difficulties for his deism but it makes it easy for him to dispose of miracles. His treatment of the topic is full of mockery, in the style of which I have just given an example, but essentially his argument comes down to this. Either a miracle is an effect of which one does not know the ultimate cause, or it is an event which contravenes the laws of nature. In the first case, everything is a miracle. We do not know the ultimate cause of attraction in physics, or vegetable growth, or anything else. In the second case, there are no miracles. It is impossible that the laws of nature should be violated. It might be suggested that God could interfere with their operation, but even if this were feasible, which Voltaire denies, why should he want to? Whatever their deficiencies, they are the best that he could contrive.

One of the best known of Voltaire's *obiter dicta* is that if there were no God it would be necessary to create him. The implication is that men can be induced to behave decently only if they expect to be rewarded or punished in an after-life. This is certainly not true of all men and I doubt if it is true of the majority. Voltaire himself has some reservations about it, as appears in the following passages from his entry on Atheism:

It is evident that, for morality, it is much better to recognize a God, than not to admit one. It is certainly in the interest of humanity that there be a God who punishes what human justice cannot repress; but it is also clear that it would be much better not to recognize a God than to worship a barbarian to whom men would be sacrificed, as has happened in the case of so many nations.

Those who have held that a society of atheists could maintain itself have been in the right, for a society is formed by its laws; and a set of atheists, being philosophers besides, can lead very sensible and happy lives in the shelter of the laws: they will certainly live more pleasantly in society than superstitious fanatics. Populate a city with men like Epicurus, Simonides, Protagoras, Desbarreau, Spinoza; populate another city with Jansenists and Molinists, in which do you think that there will be more strife and quarrels? Considered only in relation to this life, atheism would be very dangerous in a nation of savages: false notions of the Deity would not be less pernicious. Most of the great ones of this world live as if they were atheists; anyone who has had some experience of life and kept his eyes open knows that the awareness of a God, his presence, his justice, have not the slightest influence over the wars, the treaties, the objects of the ambition, interest and pleasures, which take up all these people's time; still one does not find them grossly violating the rules established in society: it is much more agreeable to pass one's life in their company than with superstitious people and fanatics. It is true that I should expect more justice from one who believes in a God than from one who does not; but I should expect only bitterness and persecution from the superstitious. Atheism and fanaticism are two monsters which can devour society and tear it asunder; but the atheist in his error preserves his reason, which cuts his claws, while the fanatic is afflicted with a continual madness which sharpens his.

We are not told where Voltaire would have us draw the line between respectable theism and superstition, though we are already in a position to suspect that he would draw it short of Christianity. He also misleads his readers in suggesting that belief in God entails belief in an after-life, whereas he himself makes no such equation. In his entry on Good and Evil, he argues that there is no better reason to suppose that men survive their death than that other animals do; indeed he goes so far as to maintain that the hypothesis of physical survival is self-contradictory. In the entry on Identity, he argues that personal continuity depends upon memory. The question then arises whether memory or indeed any other mental activity can occur independently of the body and Voltaire wishes to hold that it cannot. He quotes the opinion of Locke that it is 'not much more remote from our comprehension to conceive, that God can, if he pleases, superadd to Matter a Faculty of Thinking than that he should superadd to it another Substance, with a Faculty of Thinking.'[1] The possibility that mental properties might be shifted from one body to another did not occur to Voltaire.

If Voltaire preferred to believe that matter had the power of thought rather than that the mind or soul was a separate substance, the reason may perhaps have been that it brought him into disagreement with Descartes, to whom he is consistently hostile. So much so that in his entry on Cartesianism he lists no fewer than twenty-seven errors of which he claims that Descartes was guilty. Nearly all of them relate to particular questions of physics where Descartes's explanations were at variance with Newton's. Voltaire does, however, begin by reproaching Descartes for 'having imagined three elements which were in no way proven, after having said that one should believe nothing without proof'. Voltaire does not say what he takes these elements to have been but I suppose that he was aiming at Descartes's conception of matter as consisting in exten-

[1] *An Essay Concerning Human Understanding*, IV.3.

sion, of the self as a thinking substance and of God. Not that he rejected the certainty of Descartes's 'Cogito, ergo sum'. He himself puts the proposition that he exists and thinks on a level with mathematical certainties. What he rejected, no doubt with good reason, was the inference which Descartes drew from this primitive proposition. He was unfair to Descartes in implying that he offered no proof of the existence of God. Since, however, this proof was merely a version of the ontological argument, Voltaire was right in assuming it to be invalid.

After setting out his string of objections to Descartes's physics, Voltaire concludes his diatribe by saying: 'Finally, without going further, it will be sufficient to note that the treatment of animals in his system, lacking any physical or moral basis, or any degree of verisimilitude, has been rightly rejected not only on rational grounds but also on the simple score of sensibility.' Mainly, it would appear, for theological reasons, arising from the wish to distinguish men from other animals, not merely in degree but in kind, Descartes had characterized all other animals as unthinking and unfeeling machines. Voltaire rightly protested that this distinction between man and his fellow-creatures ran wholly counter to the empirical evidence.

I think, however, that Voltaire goes too far when he accuses both Descartes and Leibniz of being charlatans. In his entry on Charlatanism he does not mention either of them by name, but he refers both to the Cartesian theory of vortices and to Leibniz's subjection of monads to a pre-established harmony as theories which no one could sincerely hold. He fails to give Descartes credit for an ingenious attempt to accommodate motion in his account of matter or to recognize that the assumption of pre-established harmony was required by Leibniz's metaphysical premises. Voltaire was in any case disposed to reject metaphysics as nonsensical.

As an enemy to Descartes, and faithful disciple of John Locke, Voltaire cannot admit that there are innate ideas or innate principles. Consequently, he cannot allow that men's moral conscience is innate. He argues that if it were, men would all have the same moral attitudes, which they notoriously do not.

A little savage who was hungry, and to whom his father has given a piece of another savage to eat, will ask for more of the same the next day, without imagining that one should not treat one's neighbour otherwise than one would wish to be treated oneself. Mechanically, inescapably, he does the opposite of what this eternal truth enjoins.

Nature has provided for this horror; she has given man a disposition to feel pity, and the power to understand the truth. These two gifts of God are the foundations of civil society. This is why the number of cannibals has always been small; this is what makes life fairly tolerable in civilized nations. Fathers and mothers give their children an education which fits them for society; and from this education they derive a conscience.

It is typical of Voltaire's tendency to equate Nature with God, in spite of his dissociating himself from Spinoza, that he gives them both credit for endowing men with the power to apprehend moral truths and the disposition to be trained to act in accordance with them. He makes no doubt that there are moral truths, his favourite example being the principle that you should do as you would be done by, more frequently transmuted by him into its negative form that you should not do to others what you would not want them to do to you. He makes no attempt to develop a moral system but gives his approval to an amusing transcription of the gnomic sayings of Pythagoras into moral and prudential terms.

'Do not poke the fire with a sword'   That is to say 'Do not provoke angry men'.

'Abstain from beans'   'Make a habit of avoiding public assemblies [in which votes were cast with white or black beans]'.

'Do not have swallows in your house'   'Let it not be filled with chatter-boxes'.

'During storms devote yourself to the echo'   'In times of civil strife retire to the country'.

'Do not write on snow'   'Do not waste your teaching on soft and feeble minds'.

'Do not eat your heart or your brains'   'Do not give way to regret
or attempt things that are too difficult for you'.

There are some who would say that these precepts are not moral
at all, but merely prudential; but for Voltaire, as for Aristotle, whom
he joins in assenting, perhaps rather too carelessly, to the proposition
that God has implanted the knowledge of goodness in every heart,
the two were not sharply distinguished. Voltaire does not follow
Aristotle in taking happiness to be the supreme good, or indeed
in conceiving of there being a supreme good at all. He thinks the
belief in it to be one of the errors which Plato foisted on philosophers,
as part of his overall theory of Ideas. There is no more a sovereign
good than there is a sovereign square or a sovereign crimson, or
a philosopher's stone. Writing of happiness, Voltaire equates it with
pleasure and says that if one is going to view it as the greatest
good, then the greatest good is that which so delights you that
you are wholly unable to feel anything else, just as the greatest
evil will be that which deprives you of all feeling. Reverting impli-
citly to Aristotle, he says that these are the two extremes of the
human condition, and both are momentary. As for virtue, it is not
a good at all, but a duty. Again following Aristotle, more closely
perhaps than he realized, Voltaire held that behaving well was a
matter of conforming to civilized rules.

Not only did Voltaire pour scorn on Plato's theory of forms,
but in his treatment of abstract ideas he comes closer to Hume
than to Locke. At least I deduce this from his asserting in the entry
headed Ideas that the most abstract ideas are only the effects of
all the objects that one has perceived, that an idea is an image painted
in one's brain and that all one's thoughts are images. He parts company with Hume, however, in making God the painter of the picture,
remarking 'It is not I, I am not a good enough draughtsman; he
who has made me has made my ideas.' His argument here is the
same as Berkeley's, that many of my ideas come to me independently
of my own will: 'All I can do is curl them, cut them, powder them;
but it is not given to me to produce them.' Hence Voltaire is surpris-

ingly indulgent to Malebranche's doctrine that we see everything in God, though he does not go so far as to embrace it.

The fallacy of equating concepts with images has been most clearly exposed in our own day by Ludwig Wittgenstein. It would be enough to call attention to the empirical fact that we often make and understand references to all sorts of objects without conjuring up any images of them, but in case anyone is tempted to credit us with a use of latent images, there is the logical point that for an image to play its part in this affair, it needs to refer beyond itself, and to be interpreted as so doing. But if this interpretation consisted only in a reference to further images, we should be launched on an infinite regress. At some point an image needs to be directly recognized; but if an image can be recognized without an intermediary, so can the object which it was introduced to copy.

Like his master, Locke, Voltaire does not make a clear distinction between the use of the term 'idea' to designate a concept and its use to designate what many modern philosophers call a sense-datum. When it comes to sense-data he unquestioningly accepts Locke's distinction between 'ideas' of primary qualities which are resemblances of qualities that literally characterize the physical objects which are being perceived and 'ideas' of secondary qualities which are no more than powers to produce sensations in us. Colour, taste and smell are secondary qualities. The primary qualities as Locke lists them are: 'solidity, extension, figure, motion or rest, and number'. Voltaire suggests no alternative to this list.

Notoriously, Bishop Berkeley denied the validity of Locke's distinction. He claimed that extension could not be intelligibly divorced from colour. Voltaire who deals at length with Berkeley's views in his entry on Body is content to deny this proposition without argument. Of course, everyone knows that colour is no more than a sensation caused in us, but extension and solidity are intrinsic properties of external physical objects, and that is that. He then proceeds to ridicule Berkeley in robust Johnsonian fashion. 'So, according to this Doctor, ten thousand men killed by ten thousand cannon-shots are fundamentally no more than ten thousand apprehensions of our understanding; and when a man gets his wife with child, it is only one idea lodging in another idea, from which a third idea will be born.' This is an unscrupulous trading on the ambiguous usage of the term 'idea'.

Voltaire relates that when he was in England he met Berkeley and had several conversations with him. His report of them is that Berkeley based his system on the proposition that the material subject of which extension is supposed to be the attribute is inconceivable. It is because Hylas is made to assent to this that he loses the argument in his dialogues with Philonous, who is Berkeley's mouthpiece. What Voltaire would have said, in Hylas's place, is 'We know nothing about the core of this subject, nothing of this substance with its properties of extension, solidity, divisibility, mobility, figure etc.: I know it no more than I know the subject that thinks feels and wills: but this subject exists none the less because it has the essential properties of which it cannot be stripped.'

There is an echo here of Locke's characterization of substance as an 'unknown somewhat' but Voltaire's a priori handling of the problem would not have disconcerted Berkeley or, I think, satisfied Locke. If Voltaire says, as he does, that 'Berkeley's paradox is not worth the trouble it would take to refute it', it is because he fails to see the issue as a problem in the theory of knowledge. Once you follow Locke in placing the external world beyond the veil of perception, it is not at all clear how it is recoverable, any more than it is clear how one can accede to a mental subject underlying a person's state of consciousness.

In these circumstances, it is interesting to observe that, in his entry on Distance, Voltaire accepts Berkeley's theory of vision, according to which the visual field is two-dimensional, and the addition of the third dimension of depth is due to the association of the space of sight among other things with the space of touch. That these are initially distinct spaces was regarded by both Locke and Berkeley as an empirical thesis. It gave rise to Molyneux's famous problem which is stated in the following terms by Locke:

> Suppose a man *born* blind, and now adult, and taught by his *touch*
> to distinguish between a cube and a sphere of the same metal, and

nighly the same bigness, so as to tell, when he felt one and the other, which is the cube, which the sphere. Suppose then the cube and sphere be placed on the table and the blind man be made to see: *quaere*, whether *by his sight, before he touched them*, he could now distinguish and tell which is the globe, which the cube?[1]

Molyneux's own answer was 'Not' and so were Locke's and Berkeley's. Voltaire not only shares this view, but writes of it as having been empirically vindicated by a crucial experiment, carried out by the celebrated Doctor Cheselden in 1729. None the less it is still treated as an open question, at least by some contemporary psychologists.

I hope that I have said enough to show that Voltaire took a much greater interest in what is still counted as philosophy than someone who had read no further than his original Pocket Dictionary would suspect. Nevertheless he attached less importance to philosophy than to theology; if not to theological theory as such, at any rate to its practical consequences. That he did not regard philosophy, in that sense, as being of much practical consequence is shown by the last chapter of his entry on Matter, which is strongly reminiscent of Hume.

> Happily, whatever system one embraces, none of them perverts one's morals, for of what importance is it whether matter is created or arranged? God is our absolute master either way. We ought to be equally virtuous in the outcome of an organized chaos as in that of a chaos created out of nothing: hardly any of these metaphysical questions influence the conduct of our lives: these disputes are like idle table-talk: after dinner every one forgets what he has said, and goes where his interest and his taste summon him.

In his incursions into theology Voltaire is mainly concerned with Christianity and to a lesser extent with Judaism as its forerunner. He expresses admiration for Confucius, but much less for Mahomet, whom he considers to have been pretty much of a rascal with his preposterous claim to have been transported by Allah from Mecca

[1] Ibid., II.ix.8.

to Jerusalem in a single night and, more remarkably still, to have journeyed among the planets. Voltaire describes the Koran as a collection of ridiculous revelations and vague and incoherent sermons, but very good laws for the country where Mahomet lived, laws which have never been weakened or changed by interpreters of his teaching, or replaced by new decrees. His respect for these laws does not, however, extend to the means by which they have been enforced: he summarizes them as knavery and murder.

But if Voltaire can find relatively little good in Mohammedanism, he finds even less in Christianity. His objections to Christianity are partly historical and partly doctrinal. He does not attack the person of Jesus himself, though he lays some stress upon the fact that the Jewish historian, Josephus, writing in the first century AD, did not consider him worth mentioning. He also reiterates the point that there is no evidence in the Gospels or in the Pauline epistles that Jesus believed himself to be divine. The only apostle in whom Voltaire shows much interest is Saint Peter, partly because of the dispute between Peter and Paul as to the extent to which Gentile converts to Christianity should be subject to Jewish laws and customs, partly because he wished further to discredit the Papacy by exposing the fraudulence of its claim that Peter was the first Bishop of Rome. Where he begins to whet his sword is on the writings and conduct of the early Christian fathers. Most often he expresses himself ironically, but the irony is so diaphanous that it is rather a choice of style than a measure of prudence. A good example of it is to be found in the third section of the entry on Councils, a section which formed the whole of the entry in the Pocket Dictionary. I quote the opening paragraphs:

> There is no doubt that all councils are infallible: for they are composed of men.
>
> It is impossible that passions, intrigues, the spirit of contradiction, hatred, jealousy, prejudice, ignorance, should ever reign in these assemblies.
>
> But why, it will be asked, have so many councils been opposed to one another? It is to try our faith: they have all been right in their time.

Today, if one is a Roman Catholic, one believes only in the Councils of which the Vatican approves; if one is a Greek Catholic one believes only in those which enjoy the approval of Constantinople. Protestants deride them both; so everybody is happy.

We shall speak here only of the great councils; the small ones are not worth the trouble.

The first is that of Nicea. It was convoked in the year 325 of the common era, after Constantine had written this literary gem and sent it by the hand of Ozius to the rather muddle-headed clergy of Alexandria. 'You are quarrelling over a very fine point. These subtleties are unworthy of reasonable people'. The question at issue was whether Jesus was or was not created. It had nothing to do with morals, which is what matters. Whether Jesus was in time or before time, one should behave decently. After much altercation, it was at last decided that the Son was as old as the Father and *consubstantial* with the Father. This decision is hardly comprehensible; but that makes it all the more sublime. Seventeen bishops protested against the decree, and an ancient Alexandrian chronicle, preserved at Oxford, says that two thousand priests protested also; but prelates do not take much account of mere priests, who are usually poor. However that may be, there was no question of the Trinity in this first council. The formula runs: 'We believe Jesus consubstantial with the Father, God of God, light of light, begotten and not made; we believe also in the Holy Ghost.' It has to be admitted that the Holy Ghost was treated rather cavalierly.

It is reported in the supplementary proceedings of the Council of Nicea that the Fathers, not knowing how to decide which were the cryphal [sic] and which the apocryphal books of the Old and New Testaments heaped them pell-mell on an altar; the books that fell to the ground were the ones that were rejected. It is a pity that we do not still employ this excellent procedure.

After the first Council of Nicea, composed of three hundred and seventeen infallible bishops, another one was held at Rimini; and this time the number of infallible persons was four hundred, not counting a large detachment of about two hundred at Seleucia. These six hundred bishops, after four months of dispute, unanimously deprived Jesus of his *consubstantiality*. It has since been restored to him, except among Socinians: so everything is all right.

One of the great Councils is that of Ephesus in 431; the bishop of Constantinople, Nestorius, a great persecutor of heretics, was himself condemned as a heretic, for having maintained that Jesus was indeed God, but that his mother was not altogether the mother of God, but just the mother of Jesus. It was Saint Cyril who had Nestorius condemned; but the partisans of Nestorius had Saint Cyril deposed at the same council: this was very embarrassing to the Holy Ghost.

Take good note, dear reader, that there was never anything said in the Gospels either about the consubstantiality of the Word, or about the honour which Mary enjoyed in being the mother of God, or about the other disputes which led to the convocation of the infallible councils.

Voltaire goes on to describe how successive councils allotted Christ first one nature, then two, then two wills to go with the two natures, how they first condemned and then condoned the adoration of images, how a thousand bishops at a Lateran council held in 1179 put a curse on those who said that the church was too rich, how at the Council of Lyons in 1245 Cardinals were given red hats to remind them of the duty of bathing in the blood of the supporters of the Holy Roman Emperor, and how at the great Council of Constance at which Pope John XXIII was deposed for his crimes, John Huss and Jerome of Prague were burned for their obstinacy, 'given that obstinacy is a much greater crime than murder, rape, simony and sodomy'.

While Voltaire found it easy to deride the ceremony of the Eucharist, and the confusion of thought that has attended it, he was morally shocked by the doctrine of original sin. It is one of the few monstrosities of which he acquits the Jews. He traces it to Saint Augustine of Hippo, remarking that so strange an idea 'was worthy of the heated and romantic brain of a debauched and repentant African, a Manichean and a Christian, a pardoner and a persecutor, who spent his life in self-contradiction.' Voltaire puts the most forcible case against it into the mouth of a strict Unitarian.

How horrible to libel the author of nature to the extent of charging him with constant miracles for the purpose of consigning to eternal damnation men whom he brings into the world for so short a span of life. Either he has created souls for all eternity, and in that system, being infinitely older than the sin of Adam, they bear no relation to him; or these souls are formed whenever a man sleeps with a woman, and in that case God is constantly on the alert at every rendez-vous in the Universe in order to create spirits that he will render eternally unhappy; or God himself is the soul of all mankind, and in that system he damns himself. Which is the most horrible and the maddest of these three hypotheses? There isn't a fourth: for the opinion that God waits six weeks to create a damned soul in a foetus comes down to having him create it at the moment of copulation; what do six weeks matter more or less?

It is amusing to note that nowadays the opponents of abortion are more likely to believe in original sin than its advocates and that it is its advocates who believe that the six weeks do matter. But that is beside the way. What is at issue is not the time at which a foetus should be held to become a person, but the moral and intellectual depravity of the doctrine that every human being, with the solitary exception of the Virgin Mary, is born damned.

Voltaire has equally strong moral objections to the theory of grace. I quote the third section of his entry under this heading:

If someone came from the depths of hell to say to us on behalf of the devil 'Gentlemen, I notify you that my sovereign master has taken for his share the entire human race, except for a very small number of people who live around the Vatican and its dependencies,' we should all beseech this envoy to put us on the list of the privileged minority; we should ask him what one ought to do to obtain this favour.

If he replied to us: 'You can do nothing to deserve it; my master has drawn up the list for all time; he has consulted only his own whim: he is constantly engaged in making an infinite number of chamber-pots and a few dozen vessels of gold. If you are chamber-pots, so much the worse for you.'

Being treated to such a fine speech, we should pitchfork the ambassador back to his master.

All the same that is what what we have dared to impute to God, to the supremely good eternal Being.

Men have always been reproached for fashioning God in their own image. Homer was condemned for having transferred all earthly vices and absurdities to heaven. Plato, who rightly reproaches him for this, did not hesitate to call him a blasphemer. And we, a hundred times more inconsistent, rasher, more blasphemous than that Greek, who did not know how to handle the subject with finesse, we devoutly accuse God of something of which we have never accused the basest of men.

Mulei-Ismael, the king of Morocco, is said to have had five hundred children. What would you say if a Marabout from Mount Atlas told you that the wise and good Mulei-Ismael, having entertained all his family to dinner, made the following after-dinner speech:

'I am Mulei-Ismael, who have begotten you for my glory; for I am very glorious. I love you all tenderly; I care for you as a hen covers her chickens. I have decreed that one of my younger sons shall have the kingdom of Talifet, that another shall possess Morocco in perpetuity; and with regard to my other dear children, to the number of four hundred and ninety-eight, I command that half of them be broken on the wheel, and the other half burned at the stake; for I am the lord Mulei-Ismael.'

You would surely take this marabout for the uttermost madman that Africa had ever produced.

But if three or four thousand marabouts, sumptuously maintained at your expense, came and told you the same story, what would you do? Would you not be tempted to make them fast on bread and water, until they recovered their senses?

You object that I have some good reason to be indignant with the supralapsarians, who believe that the king of Morocco begot those five hundred children only for his own glory, and that he has always had the intention of causing them to be broken and burned, except for the two who were destined to reign.

But I am mistaken, you say, in attacking the infralapsarians, who maintain that Mulei-Ismael's original intention was not to have his children tortured to death; but having foreseen that they would be worthless, he considered it proper, as a good father of a family, to get rid of them by fire and on the wheel.

Ah! Supralapsarians, infralapsarians, protagonists of gratuitous, or sufficient, or efficacious grace, jansenists, molinists, be content to be men, and no longer burden the earth with your absurd and abominable follies.

The muddled thinking that has attended the doctrine of the Trinity provided Voltaire with such easy game that I forbear to list his objections to it. I note only that he credited his familiar target Saint Augustine with the following admission: 'When one asks what the three are, human language fails us, and we lack the power of expression: nevertheless we speak of three persons, not meaning anything by it, but because it is better to speak than to remain silent.'

This is just the opposite of the famous conclusion of Wittgenstein's *Tractatus*, 'Whereof one cannot speak, thereof one must be silent.' But Wittgenstein still carries an echo of Saint Augustine. I am one of those who applaud Otto Neurath's comment that in this instance there is nothing to be silent about.

I have said that Voltaire was not an atheist, but this was no thanks to Christian theology. On the contrary, he maintained that theology had driven sensible men into atheism and that philosophy had rescued them from it. I have already commented on the second of these propositions and I conclude with a quotation which endorses the first:

They debated whether the Son had been composed of two persons on earth. So the question, which went unnoticed, was whether the Deity contained five persons, counting two for Jesus-Christ on earth and three in heaven; or four persons, counting Christ on earth as only one; or three persons, considering Christ only as God. They embarked on disputes about the mother, about the descent into Hell or into Limbo, about the manner in which one ate the body of the man-God, and drank the blood of the man-God, about his grace, about his saints, and about so many other matters. When the believers in a Deity were seen to be so little in agreement among themselves, anathematizing one another, century after century, but always agreeing in their immoderate thirst for riches and honours; when on the other hand one paused to consider the prodigious amount of crime and misery with which the earth was infected, in many instances caused by the very disputes of these custodians of souls; it has to be admitted that a reasonable man was justified in doubting the existence of a being who was so strangely proclaimed, and that a sensitive man was justified in supposing that a God who had freely destined so many men for unhappiness did not exist.

6

Candide, *Zadig* and Other Tales

A curious fact about Voltaire, to which I have already drawn attention, is that although his fame has endured for over two hundred years, very little of his work is still widely read. The one great exception is the novel *Candide*, which was published in Geneva in 1759. Its full title was *Candide, ou l'optimisme*, and it was said to have been 'translated from the German of Dr Ralph, with additions found in the Doctor's pocket when he died in the year of grace 1759.' This attribution was not intended to deceive anybody and though Voltaire, as in so many other cases, disavowed the work, his authorship of it was never seriously questioned.

Candide is a satire. The optimism which is satirized approaches that described by F.H.Bradley in one of the epigrams which he inserts into the preface of his *Appearance and Reality*. There it is the doctrine that 'The World is the best of all possible worlds and everything in it is a necessary evil.' Voltaire does not go so far in *Candide* as to portray everything as evil, but the quantity of evil depicted in it vastly exceeds the quantity of good. The target at which it was actually directed is indeed the theory that this is the best of all possible worlds, with the corollary that there is a sufficient reason for all the evil that it contains. This theory was attributed to Leibniz and there is abundant evidence in his writings that he held it. Bertrand Russell suggests, in the chapter on Leibniz in his *A History of Western Philosophy*, 'that Leibniz's private inter-pretation of "the best possible world" was "the world in which the greatest number of possibilities is realized"', but it was the ethical and not the purely logical interpretation of his proposition that Leibniz publicly avowed and imparted to his followers. Voltaire also had in view the 'optimistic' lines in Pope's *An Essay on Man*:

> All nature is but art unknown to thee
> All chance, direction which thou canst not see:
> All discord, harmony not understood:
> All partial evil, universal good:
> And, spite of pride, in erring reason's spite,
> One truth is clear, Whatever is is right.

Curiously enough, this is the conclusion to which, as we have just seen, Voltaire himself appears to be committed by his combina-tion of deism and determinism. He can escape from it only by accept-ing a limitation on God's goodness or his power and, as we have also seen, he appears rather more inclined to adopt the latter course. His hostility to optimism was strongly provoked by the Lisbon earth-quake of 1755 and by Jean-Jacques Rousseau's attempt to see in it the hand of Providence. An alternative suggestion made by Vol-taire in a comment on *Candide*, of which he was then pretending not to be the author, was that God's justice was responsible for the misery that men endured in this world, but that his mercy would compensate them in the world to come. There is no doubt that this suggestion was ironical.

The story of *Candide* opens in Westphalia, in the castle of Baron Thunder-ten-tronckh. Candide is believed to be the son of the baron's sister by a gentleman of the neighbourhood whose title to nobility was insufficient for him to be allowed to marry her. The baron has a very fat wife, a son like himself, and a luscious seventeen-year-old daughter, Cunégonde. The 'oracle of the house' is the tutor Pangloss who teaches 'metaphysico-theologico-cosmonigology'. 'He succeeds admirably in proving that there is no effect without a cause, and that in this best of all possible worlds, the baron's castle is the most beautiful castle and its mistress the best possible baroness.'

Candide believes everything that his master Pangloss has told him, and loves Cunégonde, though he does not dare tell her so.

One day, Cunégonde, walking in the grounds of the castle, comes upon Doctor Pangloss in the bushes giving 'a lesson in experimental physics' to her mother's maid, a very pretty and docile little brunette. The sight so inflames Cunégonde that on the next day after dinner she lures Candide into embracing her behind a screen. The baron surprises them and literally kicks Candide out of the castle.

After wandering for a long time in the snow, tired, hungry and penniless, Candide stops at the door of an inn in a neighbouring town. Two gentlemen in blue invite him inside and give him food and drink. They ask him his height, which is five foot five, and then induce him to drink to the King of Bulgaria. When he has done so, they put his legs in irons and carry him off to a Bulgarian regiment. On the first day of training, he receives thirty strokes of a bull's pizzle, on the second, twenty and on the third only ten, so that the other conscripts think him a prodigy. When the spring comes he goes for a walk, believing it to be the privilege of members of the human species, like all other animals, to make free use of their legs. He has not gone far before he is arrested, tried and given the choice of running the gauntlet of the regiment thirty-six times or receiving twelve lead bullets in his brain. The strength of the regiment is two thousand men. Candide opts for the gauntlet but after two runs decides that he would prefer to be shot. He has already been blindfolded when the King of Bulgaria comes upon the scene and learning that Candide is a young metaphysician reprieves him. An able surgeon cures Candide of his wounds in three weeks, just in time for him to take part in the battle which the King of the Bulgarians has joined against the King of the Abarians.

The two armies are well matched. Six thousand men on each side perish in the opening cannonade; then the musketry removes nine or ten thousand rascals from the best of worlds; the bayonet accounts with sufficient reason for several thousand more. In all, the losses amount to some thirty thousand souls. Candide, with a philosopher's prudence, takes cover during the slaughter. Afterwards, while each king is having a *Te Deum* sung in his camp, Candide visits first an Abarian and then a Bulgarian village. Each has been burned, in accordance with international law. In each of them, old men have been savagely beaten, women are dying with their throats cut, girls have been raped and disembowelled. The countryside is in ruins. In the confusion Candide makes good his escape.

Arriving in Holland as a beggar, Candide is rudely rebuffed, until a good Anabaptist, called Jacques, has pity on him, takes him into his house, gives him bread and beer and a little money and offers him employment in his manufactory of Persian fabrics. The next day Candide, out walking, gives the money to a beggar who is horribly disfigured. When he recoils from the beggar's embrace, the beggar says 'Do you not recognize your dear Pangloss?' Candide takes Pangloss into Jacques's stable, gives him some bread and at once asks after Cunégonde. Pangloss replies that she is dead. Candide wonders if she has died for love of him. Pangloss says No, she has been disembowelled by Bulgarian soldiers, after being repeatedly raped, her brother likewise, the baron and baroness both murdered. And how has Pangloss got into such a wretched state? Through love. He has caught syphilis from Paquette, the baroness's maid, who had caught it from a learned Franciscan, who had caught it from an old countess, who had caught it from a cavalry captain, who owed it to a marchioness, who had it from a page, who had got it from a Jesuit who, as a novice, had caught it directly from one of the company of Christopher Columbus. Candide exclaims that the devil must have been at the root of such a tree. But Pangloss will not desert his principle. It is a necessary ingredient in the best of worlds. For instance, if Columbus had not introduced this scourge into the Old World, we should not have the benefit of chocolate or cochineal.

Its moral being thus established, the story continues at considerable length in a similar vein. The good Jacques, who has taken Candide and Pangloss with him on a voyage to Lisbon, perishes in a tidal wave which precedes the Lisbon earthquake. Pangloss, who has been cured of syphilis at the cost of an eye and an ear and the tip of his nose, proves that Lisbon harbour has been expressly designed for Jacques to be drowned in it. He falls foul, however, of the Inquisition for appearing to deny the doctrine of original sin; for if everything is for the best the fall and its punishment cannot have taken place. Pangloss's claim that man's fall and the curse laid upon him enters necessarily into the best of possible worlds provokes the charge that he denies man's freedom. His attempt to argue that we are necessarily free is cut short and he is sentenced to be hanged. Candide is sentenced to be whipped in cadence with an anthem for seeming to agree with him.

Candide's whipping is witnessed by Cunegónde who has been given a front seat at the *auto de fe*. Having been no more than wounded by the Bulgarian troops, she had been sold to a Jew who set her up in his country house, only to be obliged to share her company with the Grand Inquisitor. Cunégonde despatches the Jew's servant, an old woman, to bring Candide to her. The old woman, the daughter of a Pope and a Princess, has had her own full share of troubles, including the loss of a buttock which served as food for soldiers undergoing a siege. After making love, Candide and Cunégonde are surprised first by the Jew and then by the Inquisitor both of whom Candide kills. Consequently, they and the old woman, flee to Cadiz and take ship for the New World. They are betrayed by a Franciscan's theft of Cunégonde's jewellery which is traced back to the Inquisitor when the Franciscan tries to sell it and is hanged as a result. A ship is sent to Buenos Aires to arrest Candide. He is forced to abandon Cunégonde to the Governor of Buenos Aires and sets out with his faithful servant, the half-caste Peruvian, Cacambo, to offer their services to the Jesuits in Paraguay against whom an expedition has been organized by the Pope.

When they reach Paraguay they discover that the Commander of the Jesuit forces is none other than Cunégonde's brother whom the Bulgarians had also not succeeded in killing. He was on the point of being buried in a Jesuit chapel when he showed signs of life and was recruited into the Jesuit order. He receives Candide very warmly until Candide declares his intention of marrying Cunégonde. Infuriated by such presumption the young baron strikes Candide who runs him through. Candide then disguises himself in the baron's Jesuit costume and makes his escape with Cacambo.

After various adventures, including an encounter with savages who refrain from eating them only when they discover that Candide is not really a Jesuit, Candide and Cacambo descend by chance upon the earthly paradise of El Dorado, the ancient land of the Incas, protected by high mountains from the outside world. It is a benevolent monarchy, with no law courts or prisons, fantastically prosperous, to the point where the children play quoits with rubies, diamonds and pieces of gold. The ruler presses them to stay but Candide still hankers after Cunégonde and also relishes the prospect of the power which the riches bestowed on him in El Dorado will permit him to enjoy. He and Cacambo are hoisted over the mountains with a hundred red sheep laden with treasures, but only two of the sheep survive the long and perilous journey to the Dutch colony of Surima and these two are stolen from Candide by a Dutch sea captain.

Candide and Cacambo still have their pockets full of gold and diamonds and Candide sends Cacambo off to Buenos Aires with money enough to purchase Cunégonde from the Governor and bring her to Venice where he will meet them. Candide himself embarks on a French ship with a new companion, Martin, whose personal misfortunes together with years of working for publishers in Amsterdam, have turned him into a Manichean, the very opposite of Pangloss, believing that everything is for the worst.

The French ship has not proceeded far on its way to Bordeaux before it encounters the Dutch ship, carrying Candide's sheep, engaged in battle with a Spanish vessel. The Dutchman is sunk, which causes Candide to say that it serves the captain right. But what of the innocent passengers, asks Martin. The only survivor is one of Candide's sheep, shorn of its treasures. Candide presents it to the Academy of Sciences in Bordeaux.

From Bordeaux, Candide and Martin make their way to Paris where Candide is able to experience all the frivolity and malice of the best society. He is cheated at cards, unfaithful to Cunégonde with a marchioness who appropriates two of his largest diamonds and robbed by an Abbé and his accomplice, a woman masquerading as Cunégonde. The Abbé contrives to have Candide and Martin arrested but by bribing the police they regain their freedom in Dieppe. There they embark for Portsmouth, where they stay just long enough to witness the English carrying out their custom of shooting an admiral from time to time 'to encourage the others'. Candide then secures them passages to Venice.

In Venice they fail to find Cacambo or Cunégonde. Instead they come across Paquette, the maid who had given Pangloss syphilis. She has adopted the career of a prostitute and her latest client is a Theatine monk called Giroflée. Candide gives them money for which, as Martin has predicted, they are not grateful. When Cacambo finally meets Candide in Venice, he tells him that Cunégonde, still with the old woman, is in Constantinople and warns him that she has grown very ugly. It had taken him half the money that he had brought from El Dorado to obtain her release from the Governor of Buenos Aires and he had been robbed of the rest by a pirate who had taken them from port to port and finally dumped them at Scutari. Cunégonde was washing dishes in the service of an exiled Prince of Transylvania and Cacambo had come to Venice as the slave of a deposed Turkish sultan. After supping with this former sultan and five other deposed and indignant sovereigns, Candide and Martin embark upon the ship which is taking Cacambo and his master back to Turkey. Candide ransoms not only Cacambo but also Pangloss and the young baron whom he finds rowing as galley slaves on the vessel to which he and Martin have exchanged at the entrance to the Black Sea. Pangloss's hangman had been incompetent and Pangloss had come to when a surgeon barber was dissecting him. The barber sewed him up and he eventually entered into the employment of a Venetian merchant who took him to Constantinople. There he had been arrested, suffered the bastinado and condemned to the galleys for returning her corsage to a lady in a mosque. The baron, whom Candide had only wounded, was imprisoned in Buenos Aires at about the time his sister left it, rejoined his order in Rome and was sent to Constantinople as a Jesuit almoner. His crime, for which he had suffered the same punishment as Pangloss, had been to bathe naked with a young Muslim.

When Candide has duly ransomed Cunégonde, together with the old woman, he finds that she has indeed grown so ugly that he no longer desires to marry her. He is provoked into doing so by the opposition of her brother who continues to object to Candide's lack of nobility. The baron makes himself such a nuisance that Candide ships him back to the galley with instructions that he shall be returned to the Jesuits in Italy. The rest of the party settles down on a small-holding in Turkey, where they are joined by Paquette and Giroflée. Soon this is all that they have, since the Jews cheat Candide out of what is left of his fortune. For a time they are bored and discontented. Cunégonde, growing uglier every day, becomes a shrew. The old woman's temper is no better. Cacambo complains of having to grow vegetables and sell them in Constantinople. Candide disputes with his two philosophers.

A visit to a local dervish does nothing for them, but they are saved by the example of a local fruit-grower, an old man who cares nothing for public affairs, but is fully occupied with his sons and daughters in making the most of his property. Once Candide decides to imitate him, all goes well. Cunégonde is really very ugly but she becomes a good pastry-cook. Paquette sews; the old woman takes charge of the linen; even Giroflée contributes. He is an excellent carpenter and becomes a decent fellow.

> Pangloss sometimes says to Candide 'All these events are strung together in the best of possible worlds: for after all, if you had not been kicked out of a fine castle for love of Mademoiselle Cunégonde, if you had not been subjected to the Inquisition, if you had not walked all over America, if you had not run the baron through with your sword, it you had not lost all your sheep from the good country of El Dorado, you would not be here eating candied lemons and pistachios.' 'That is very well said,' replies Candide, 'but we must cultivate our garden.'

Zadig is the longest of the 'philosophical tales' that Voltaire composed in 1747 while staying with Madame du Châtelet at the country house of the Duchesse de Maine. It is a picaresque story, less eventful than *Candide* and with a smaller cast of characters. There is no discernible moral to it, except towards the end where an angel, appearing to Zadig in the guise of a hermit, carries out a series of what appear to be perverse and even villainous actions, such as drowning a boy of fourteen whose aunt had shown them hospitality. In this instance, when Zadig remonstrates with the hermit, he is told that the boy would have assassinated his aunt in a year's time and Zadig himself a year after that. When Zadig asked why the boy had to be endowed with such a bad character, the angel replied that if the boy had been virtuous and had lived, his destiny was to be assassinated together with the wife whom he was fated to marry and the son whom he was fated to beget. Some time previously Zadig had dissuaded a fisherman from committing suicide, and he is told that the supreme being, Orosmade, had sent him to change the fisherman's destiny.

Perhaps fidelity to logic should not be demanded of a fable, but Voltaire intended his stories to carry a philosophical message, and here the message is confused. If something is destined to happen, then *ex hypothesi* nothing can prevent it. The notion of interfering with destiny is self-contradictory, a point on which we have seen that Voltaire himself relies when he denies the possibility of miracles. There is a suggestion that the future can be directed by some outside intervention along one or other of an alternative set of fatal paths, but this is inconsistent with the overall determinism which Voltaire elsewhere espouses. It is inconsistent also with the rather strange cosmology in which Zadig is instructed in the same paragraph. In reply to his question 'What if there were only good and no evil?' the angel is made to answer:

In that case this earth would be a different earth; the series of events would exhibit a different order of wisdom; and this different order, which would be perfect, could exist only in the eternal dwelling of the Supreme Being, which evil cannot approach. He has created millions of worlds no one of which can resemble any other. This immense variety is characteristic of his immense power. There are no two leaves of a tree on earth, or two globes in the infinite expanses of the sky, that are alike; and everything that you see on this little atom where you were born, was bound to be in its fixed place and time, according to the immutable laws of him who encompasses everything... there is no such thing as chance: everything is a test, or a punishment, or a reward, or a prevision.

Here Voltaire seems to have borrowed Leibniz's principle of the identity of indiscernibles and taken it to extravagant lengths. It is not clear how millions of different worlds can intelligibly be thought to co-exist. Nor how room can be found for reward and punishment in a deterministic scheme which also carries the burden of providence. It is remarkable also to find Voltaire accepting the principle of sufficient reason, another legacy from Leibniz, which he so effectively satirizes in *Candide*. There is, however, the difference of date to be considered. It may well be that Voltaire's assessment of Leigniz's philosophy changed for the worse between 1747 and 1759.

Unlike Candide, Zadig is neither an innocent, nor much of a victim. He is indeed encumbered with a series of misfortunes, but he is shown as triumphing over them, mainly through his sagacity. From the start he is represented as young, handsome, learned, virtuous and rich. He enjoys consideration in Babylon where the story is originally set. He is engaged to be married first to a princess and then to a lady of lower degree, but in both cases discovers in time that they do not love him. He wins the esteem of the king and queen by an impressive exercise in detection: he derives a detailed description of a runaway horse and lost spaniel from the traces which they have left in the road beside his house.

After a display of moral courage, Zadig is made Prime Minister. His administration is wise and popular, but by a trick similar to that by which Iago entraps Othello, an enemy of Zadig's persuades the king that his wife, Astarte, is deceiving him with Zadig. This is not true, though Zadig and Astarte are in love with one another. The king plans to kill them both but they are warned in time. Astarte takes refuge in a monastery and Zadig flees to Egypt. There is a slight foretaste of *Candide* in the account of Zadig's first adventure in Egypt. He comes upon a man savagely beating a woman, fights a duel with the man and kills him, only to be bitterly reproached by the woman, Missouf, for depriving her of her lover. A party of men from Babylon mistake Missouf for Astarte and carry her off to their king, who becomes enamoured of her and makes her his queen. Her caprices throw the kingdom into confusion; there is a civil war and an invasion by a neighbouring prince who kills the king and captures both Astarte and Missouf. Astarte escapes with the connivance of Missouf, only to be captured by a brigand and sold by him to a sybarite.

Meanwhile Zadig, in accordance with the laws of Egypt, has been condemned to slavery for manslaughter. His intelligence, however, soon procures him the confidence of his master. They travel to Arabia where Zadig dissuades a young widow from immolating herself on her husband's pyre, thereby setting a precedent which puts an end to this custom in Arabia. After various adventures preceding his meeting with the fisherman, Zadig has the good fortune to come upon the estate of the sybarite who is holding Astarte captive. The sybarite fancies that he is ill and Zadig purchases Astarte's freedom by promising to cure him. He does so by making him take exercise.

Astarte returns to Babylon to find that her partisans are in a position to restore her to the throne. A combination of a physical and an intellectual exercise is held to choose her consort. Zadig is successful in both parts, though he has to engage in an additional fight when the armour in which he has won the tournament is stolen from him. The intellectual exercise consists partly in answering riddles. Two examples are given. The first runs: 'Of everything in the world which is the longest and the shortest, the fastest and the slowest, the most divisible and the most extended, the most neglected and the most regretted, that without which nothing can be done, that which devours everything small and gives life to whatever is great?' Zadig's answer is 'Time'. To the second question 'What is the thing that one receives without giving thanks, enjoys without knowing how, gives to others when one is transported out of oneself, and loses without noticing?', his answer is 'Life'.

These answers, among others, contribute to Zadig's triumph;

and he and Astarte are depicted, as in a fairy-tale, as reigning bliss-fully thereafter.

If the merits of *Zadig* hardly equal those of *Candide*, Voltaire's other tales are very slight. *Le Monde comme il va* (How the World Goes) is a comment on French and especially Parisian customs, disguised as a criticism of Persia. The Scythian Babouc is ordered by the genie Ituriel to visit Persia and return with a report, as a result of which Ituriel will decide whether Persepolis is to be reformed or destroyed. Babouc begins by witnessing a bloody battle fought between the Persian and Indian armies in a war which was started for some very trivial reason. He is shocked by the brutality of the troops and the neglect of the wounded in the military hospitals. He is, however, disposed to be reassured by the declaration of peace.

Babouc enters Persepolis, that is to say, Paris, by way of the most ancient quarter of the city which he finds offensively ugly and decrepit. He follows a crowd into a church, which he begins by mistaking for a furniture shop. He discovers his mistake when he observes women on their knees, ostensibly at prayer but covertly glancing at the men by their side. The chanting that he hears so resembles the braying of asses that he has to stop his ears. What disgusts him most of all is that burials take place in the church. He regards this as a source of pestilence.

In the afternoon Babouc goes to dine at the other end of town, in the house of a lady to whom her husband, an army officer, had given him a letter of introduction. On his way there, he is impressed by the architecture, including that of many churches, the handsome squares, the magnificent bridges over the river, the numerous foun-tains, the civility of the inhabitants. The house at which he is enter-tained is clean and well-furnished, the meal delicious, his hostess young, beautiful, witty and attractive, the company worthy of her. He thinks it ridiculous of the angel Ituriel to want to destroy such a charming city.

His good opinion of the company was, however, changed when his hostess confessed to him that she was having an affair with a young priest, and added that this was customary among her friends. He was shocked also to discover that a young man, to whom

CANDIDE, ZADIG AND OTHER TALES

an elderly lawyer was showing deference, had purchased the office of a judge. Nor was he appeased when a young soldier assured him that commissions in the army were also purchased. He took further exception to the behaviour of one of the 'plebeian kings' who made fortunes out of collecting the taxes of the empire.

After dinner Babouc attended a service at which he was bored but not offended by the sermon and then went to a theatre where such noble sentiments were so eloquently expressed that he mistook the players for preachers. When he called upon the principal actress he found her ill-lodged and poorly dressed. She complained that she was paid so little that she could not afford to have the child that she was carrying. Babouc gave her some money and then visited a fashionable shop at which he bought some trinkets at much more than their value. When the friend with whom he was staying convinced him that he had been swindled, he put down the merchant on the list of those whom Ituriel should make sure of punishing. Shortly afterwards the merchant called to return Babouc's purse which Babouc had left behind in the shop. Babouc complimented him on this piece of honesty but reproached him for selling him goods at four times their value. Not four times, replied the merchant, but ten times. He then explained that every reputable merchant would have returned Babouc's purse but that they would all have sought an equally large profit from the baubles that they were selling. He then launched into a defence of the capitalist system. Babouc was sufficiently impressed to remove the merchant's name from his black-list.

Babouc next paid a visit to a convent where he noted that the vows of poverty and humility had not prevented the 'archimandrite' from acquiring considerable wealth and power. The rumour that Babouc was an inspector led the inmates to exalt their own convent at the expense of all the rest. He had hit upon the equivalent of Jansenists and was shocked to find them at odds with the Grand Lama, or, in other words, the Pope.

Disillusioned with the clergy, he entered into the company of men of letters, whom he discovered to be more openly vain, quarrelsome and hostile to one another than the priests. He read some of their productions which he found full of malice and devoid of taste. Later, however, he came across an elderly man of letters who kept aloof from the herd; this man was joined by a friend and Babouc found their conversation interesting and instructive. He concluded that the literature of Persepolis was not wholly contemptible. He learned also that there were some estimable men among the Jansenists, that the officers who purchased their commissions fought bravely, and that the young judges who had purchased their appointments rendered sensible verdicts whereas the elderly lawyers lost themselves in pedantic quibbles.

Babouc was still disturbed by the morals of what passed for the best society. However when he visited a powerful minister he discovered that the hostess whose dalliance with the priest had shocked him was ardently and in the end successfully pleading her husband's cause. He learned that the lady was on the best of terms with her husband and with her husband's mistress, just as her husband looked favourably upon the young priest. He was invited to sup with the four of them and spent a most pleasant evening. He was told of a hostess, on similar terms with her husband, who kept an admirable salon. The reference is almost certainly to Voltaire's mistress, Madame du Châtelet.

At this point Babouc concluded that good and bad in Persepolis were inextricably mixed. In order to make his report to Ituriel he had the best sculptor in Persepolis cast a statue in which all metals, clays, and the most precious and worthless stones were mingled. He then proposed to say to Ituriel 'Would you destroy this pretty statue because it is not wholly made of gold and diamonds?' In response, Ituriel decided to let things go on as they were.

Voltaire concludes his tale as follows:

So Persepolis was allowed to survive: and Babouc was far from complaining, unlike Jonah who was angry that Nineveh was not destroyed. But when one has spent three days in the belly of a whale, one is not in so good a mood as when one has been to the opera and the theatre and supped in good company.

These are the most important of Voltaire's tales. There are many others but none is worth recounting in detail. *Le Crocheteur borgne* is like a story of the *Arabian Nights* in which the one-eyed porter of the title dreams of being transformed into a handsome gallant who saves the life and enjoys the favours of a beautiful princess. The heroine of *Cosi-Sancta*, having rejected, out of a sense of duty, the advances of a would-be lover, whom her jealous husband murders none the less, saves her husband's life by yielding to the judge, her brother's life by yielding to the chief of a company of bandits, and her son's life by yielding to the only doctor competent to cure him. The moral of the story is that it is worth committing a small evil, like marital infidelity, to obtain a great good. The hero of *Memnon* resolves to lead an entirely sensible life; he will have nothing to do with women; he will be careful to stay sober; he has money safely invested with the receiver-general of the finances of Nineveh so that he need not seek a patron at court. Having so resolved, he is immediately enticed by an adventuress whose 'uncle' surprises them and extorts a large sum of money from him. To console himself for this loss he accepts an invitation to dine with some of his closest friends, gets drunk, gambles, loses all the money that he had on him and more, and has an eye put out by a dice box which one of his friends throws at him. When he applies to the receiver-general for money to pay his gambling-debts he learns that he has gone bankrupt. He goes for redress to the King of Babylon who refers him to a satrap. The satrap is a patron of the defaulting financier and threatens Memnon with the loss of his remaining eye. An angel then visits him and tells him that he is better off than his elder brother, a courtier in an Indian state whose sovereign has had him blinded and put in prison. Memnon obtains from the angel the assurance that this is not quite the worst of worlds, but this does not console him for the loss of his eye.

The theme of a multiplicity of worlds governs the very short story of *Le Rêve de Platon* (Plato's dream). Voltaire can seldom refrain from mocking Plato and after alluding to the fantasy, attributed to Aristophanes in the *Symposium*, that men and women seek the other halves of the wholes which they originally formed, he derides Plato for the suggestion that there can be only five perfect worlds, corresponding to the five regular solids in mathematics. The dream is that 'the great Geometer' convokes all the demiurges who have ordered affairs in different planets. The demiurge who has contrived the Earth is mercilessly ridiculed but the organizer of Mars is unable to show that he has done any better. The Eternal Demiurge sums up:

> You have [he told them] created good and bad things, because you are highly intelligent, but imperfect: your works will last only for some hundred millions of years; after that, having learned more, you will do better: it is only my province to create what is perfect and eternal.
>
> That is what Plato taught his disciples. When he had stopped speaking, one of them said 'And then you woke up.'

Jeannot et Colin is a moral tale of two boys from the Auvergne. Jeannot is the son of a muleteer, Colin the son of a farm-labourer. The boys are friends until Jeannot's father succeeds in business and transforms himself into Monsieur le Marquis de la Jeannotière, whereupon Jeannot, now a young marquis, drops Colin. The tutor whom Jeannot's parents engage for him in Paris persuades them that it is not necessary for him to be taught anything except how to love. The young Marquis is a social success and becomes engaged to a widow of quality. Suddenly, his father is ruined and imprisoned for debt, the widow disowns him, his grand friends turn their backs on him, he is not equipped to earn his own living. By chance he meets Colin who is happily married to the daughter of a prosperous merchant and has risen to be manager of a plate and copper works. Colin greets Jeannot as an old friend, pays off his father's creditors and takes him into his business. Jeannot, whom society has not wholly corrupted, marries Colin's sister. The moral is that vanity does not make for happiness.

Micromégas, owing something to Swift's *Gulliver's Travels*, is the tale of a giant from one of the planets of Sirius who travels to the planet Saturn and there makes friends with a much smaller creature, who is himself a giant by our standards. The two of them repair to earth where they manage to communicate with creatures who seem to them so small as to be incorporeal. Micromégas addresses them as intelligent atoms and falsely supposes them to spend their lives in love and thought, remarking that these constitute the true life of the spirit and the only genuine sources of happiness. Here I believe that Voltaire was speaking for himself.

7

'Écrasez l'infâme'

Jean Calas was a prosperous merchant of Toulouse. He owned a clothier's shop in the rue des Filatiers and lived above it with his wife, six children, and a servant Jeanne Viguier who in 1761 had been with the family for twenty-five years. At that date Jean Calas was 62 years old, and his wife, an Englishwoman born Rose Cabibel, eighteen years younger. The children, of whom there were four boys and two girls, ranged in age from the eldest son Marc-Antoine, who was 28, to the youngest son Donat who was 15 and apprenticed to a clothiers in Nîmes. Only the second son Pierre and the two daughters Rosine and Nanette assisted in Calas's shop.

Ever since the war against the Albigenses had ended in a Catholic victory at the beginning of the thirteenth century, Toulouse had been a centre of religious tension. On 17 May 1562, ten years before the massacre of Saint Bartholemew, four thousand Huguenots had been murdered, after being induced by the promise of a safe-conduct to lay down their arms. Two hundred years later the anniversary of this crime was commemorated annually by a procession of the vainglorious Catholics.

The Calas family was Protestant. They had never suffered for their faith, except that Jean Calas and his wife when they were newly married had been prevented from emigrating to England. Nor were they militant in their Protestantism. Their faithful servant was a Catholic and when their third son Louis became converted to Catholicism and chose to live apart from the remainder of the family, his father did not disown him but gave him financial support.

The eldest son caused his parents concern. An intelligent and hard-working young man, well read in the classics, he was also moody, theatrical and a gambler. He had taken a degree in law in 1759 and wished to practise at the Toulouse bar. For this he required a certificate of religious orthodoxy from his parish priest. He took the precaution of having himself baptized into the Roman Catholic church but was still denied his certificate because he was unable to show that he had ever subjected himself to confession. After this he became increasingly melancholy and dissipated. His father did not consider him fitted either by his tastes or character for a partnership in his business.

On 13 October 1761, Louis Calas having left home and the two daughters being away in the country, five people supped at the Calas's house. In addition to the parents, they were the eldest son Marc-Antoine, his brother Pierre and a friend of Pierre's called Gaubert Lavaysse, whose father, although a Protestant, was a successful barrister in Toulouse. Jeanne Viguier served the meal. Marc-Antoine ate little and left early telling Jeanne that he did not feel well. About half past nine Pierre and Gaubert left for a walk in time for Gaubert to return to his house. When they went downstairs they found Marc-Antoine's body hanging from a wooden beam. They cut him down and called a doctor who pronounced him dead. It was clear that he had committed suicide. When Jean Calas was alerted, he instructed the young men to say no more than that they had discovered the corpse. His reason was that it was then the custom in Toulouse for suicides to be stripped naked, placed face downwards on a hurdle and dragged through the streets and he wished his son's body to be spared this indignity. This paternal sentiment was fatal to him.

A crowd gathered and someone cried out that Marc-Antoine had been murdered by his family because he had told them of his conversion to Catholicism. There was no evidence at all in favour of this proposition and considerable evidence against it. Ever since he had been denied his barrister's certificate Marc-Antoine had become more outspokenly Protestant; his body showed no signs of the struggle that must have taken place if he had been strangled by members of his family: in that event they would hardly have proceeded immediately to call their neighbours' attention to his death: they would have been more likely to affirm that he had committed suicide than to deny it. Their acquiescence in the conversion of their third son and their long employment of a Catholic servant showed that they were not Protestant bigots.

This absurd accusation might have had no serious effect, had it not been for the presence in the crowd of the titular Capitoul of Toulouse, David de Beaudrigue. By long tradition, Toulouse came under the local government of eight 'Capitouls'. One, the titular, purchased the office and held it for life; the other seven were periodically elected. Their duties included serving as magistrates. De Beaudrigue was a fanatical upholder of the established order. Without even bothering to satisfy the formality of obtaining a legal warrant, he arrested all the members of the household together with Gaubert Lavaysse. The three men remained in prison for the next five months. A lawyer was assigned to them but he was not permitted to bring forward any witnesses or indeed cite any evidence in their defence. The only admission that the inquisitors could obtain from Jean Calas under torture was that he had concealed the fact that his son had committed suicide.

The case was effectively prejudged in the first week of November when the body of Marc-Antoine was buried with Catholic pomp. A company of the White Penitents accompanied the cortège to the cathedral where a requiem mass was held. Two days later the White Penitents conducted another service 'for the soul of the martyr' in their own chapel. Nevertheless, it was not until 9 March 1762 that the judges, by a majority of eight to five, found Jean Calas guilty of murdering his eldest son. He was sentenced to be broken on the wheel, to be allowed a further period, in effect two hours, for repentance and confession, then to be strangled and his body cremated. Two-thirds of his property was forfeit to the state. Sentence on the other defendants was suspended.

Jean Calas underwent his sentence on the following day. He bore the torture inflicted on him with great fortitude and protested his innocence until the moment of his death. His bearing is said to have caused many of the spectators to become doubtful of his guilt.

This doubt was reflected in the sentences passed on 19 March upon the other suspects. Pierre Calas was sentenced to be banished from the city, Madam Calas and Gaubert Lavaysse were non-suited. Jeanne Viguier was acquitted. The inconsistency with the sentence passed on Jean Calas was glaring. It was patent that if Jean Calas had strangled Marc-Antoine it could have been only with the connivance and indeed the active assistance of Pierre Calas and his friend. Why then were they not condemned to the same punishment? In fact the sentence pronounced on Pierre Calas was not executed. Instead he was confined for four months in a Dominican monastery in Toulouse.

Another inconsistency was shown in the treatment of the Calas daughters, who had not even been at home on the night of their brother's death. The Secretary of State, Monsieur de Saint-Florentin, who throughout the affair was inclined to take the side of the Toulouse magistrates, was persuaded to issue *lettres de cachet* confining the girls to separate convents for seven months. Neither of them underwent conversion, though the younger gained the respect and affection of the nuns, one of whom wrote a letter to a highly placed relative of hers in Paris, saying that the girl's character and the account she gave of her family had convinced her of their innocence.

The case was brought to Voltaire's attention by a friend, M. Audibert, who had been in Toulouse shortly after Jean Calas's execution and believed that it had been a miscarriage of justice. Voltaire was at first unsure. The inquiries which he caused to be made through the Cardinal de Bernis and the Duc de Richelieu were inconclusive. By some early date, however, young Donat Calas must have found his way to Ferney and made a favourable impression on Voltaire. At all events, in a letter to d'Alembert, dated 29 March 1762, Voltaire writes as one who is almost wholly convinced of Calas's innocence. His letter crossed a letter from d'Alembert, written to him from Paris on 31 March, in which d'Alembert not only takes Jean

159

Calas's innocence for granted, but refers also to an earlier outrage at Toulouse when a Protestant pastor had been executed for attempting to baptize a child in secret. D'Alembert's comment on the two cases was that not all the inquisitors are at Lisbon.

By 4 April Voltaire was sufficiently persuaded to write a letter to M. Damilaville, for circulation to his fellow *Encyclopédistes*, in which he speaks of its having been ascertained without doubt that the judges of Toulouse had caused an innocent man to be broken on the wheel, and begs his correspondents to make this fact widely known. He also formed a committee of sympathizers in Geneva to assist him in his effort to get the case reviewed. If he himself had any lingering doubts about the merits of the case they were removed by the arrival at Ferney in July of Pierre Calas who had succeeded in escaping from the Dominican monastery in Toulouse. Voltaire questioned Pierre Calas closely and was confirmed in his belief that there had been a gross miscarriage of justice.

Voltaire's campaign very largely depended upon his ability to obtain the support of persons in power. So we find the Marquise de Pompadour writing to the Duc de Fitzjames, towards the end of August 1762, to say that the sympathy of the King had been enlisted and that although the poor man, Jean Calas, cannot be brought back to life 'all France cries out for vengeance'. The powerful Duc de Choiseul was also favourably disposed, but he was offended by a doctored version of Voltaire's letter of 29 March to d'Alembert, reproduced at face value in an English newspaper, in which Voltaire was caused to appear to make disparaging references to the French king and his ministers. Fortunately d'Alembert had kept Voltaire's letter to him; the fraud was exposed, and the Duc de Choiseul was appeased.

Meanwhile the magistrates at Toulouse remained obdurate. They would not consider the possibility of their having been in error; and when at a later stage they were required to furnish Madame Calas with copies of the documents on the case they refused to do so except at an exorbitant cost. Voltaire's only recourse was to have the verdict of the Toulouse court annulled on technical grounds by the King's Council and a fresh trial of the four survivors,

Madame Calas, Pierre Calas, Gaubert Lavaysse and Jeanne Viguier held in Paris. The first step towards this end was to induce the King's Council to accept a petition, on behalf of the Calas family, for a reconsideration of the case. With the help of three eminent lawyers this was achieved on 7 March 1763. After that everything was plain sailing, although it was not until June 1764 that the King's Council annulled the judgements passed by the Toulouse court on Jean Calas and the other accused, and not until 9 March 1765 that all the surviving defendants were formally acquitted and the memory of Jean Calas legally vindicated. An order was given that everything relating to the guilt of the accused, including the report of their arrests, should be expunged from the Toulouse court records, but it would seem that this order was never carried out. Indeed there were many in Toulouse who persisted in believing in Jean Calas's guilt. They probably did not include David de Beaudrigue who went mad and committed suicide.

The question was raised whether Madame Calas should try to obtain compensation from the Toulouse authorities, but the state of opinion in Toulouse and the cost of the attempt made this seem inadvisable. The King gave a grant to her and to the members of her family, but it was not enough to restore them to their former prosperity. Primarily the case was a moral victory for Voltaire.

Voltaire associated the Calas case with that of Pierre-Paul Sirven, another Protestant who lived at Mazamet in the province of Langue-doc. Sirven, a surveyor, had a wife and three daughters of whom the eldest was married and one of her younger sisters thought to be feeble-minded. This girl was called Elizabeth. In March 1760 Elizabeth disappeared. After he had spent a day searching for her, her father was summoned to the palace of the Bishop of Castres and informed that his daughter, over whom the Bishop's sister had some influence, had taken refuge there as a would-be Catholic con-vert and had been sent to the nunnery of the Black Ladies. Sirven regretted the loss of his daughter but raised no objection to the course which the Bishop had taken.

Elizabeth had not been long in the nunnery of the Black Ladies before she went mad. The nuns kept her with them for seven months, and then returned her home, where her madness continued. Sirven accused the nuns of driving the girl mad, and they accused him of maltreating her because of her desire to be converted. Once again she disappeared and remained missing for a fortnight. Some children then discovered her body in a well. At first no one doubted that she had committed suicide.

But then, as in the Calas case, rumours began to circulate. Was it not notorious that Protestants murdered their children to prevent their conversion to Catholicism? Pierre-Paul Sirven had not been at home on the night that Elizabeth disappeared, so that suspicion fell first upon his wife and then on one of his daughters. If they were guilty, they might have been acting on his instructions. It came to the point where their friends advised the Sirvens that it was not safe for them to remain at home. In the winter of 1762 the father made his way on foot to Lausanne; the women hid in Nîmes.

Judicial action was taken against the family. It proceeded slowly, complicated by the fact that Elizabeth's corpse was stolen. Sentence was eventually passed in 1764. Monsieur and Madame Sirven were condemned to be hanged. The two surviving daughters were to witness the execution of their parents and then be banished. Five months were spent in a vain effort to trace the Sirvens. The father and mother were then hanged in effigy in the principal square of Mazamet.

The Sirven case was brought to Voltaire's notice by the Geneva pastor Moulton, who had already supported him in the affair of Calas. When Sirven begged Voltaire for help, it was at once accorded. Since the verdict had been delivered by a minor judge, the appeal had to be made in the first instance to the magistrature of Toulouse. Fortunately, its composition had changed since the time of the Calas trial. Even so, Voltaire encountered many obstacles which he doggedly overcame. By the end of 1765 Pierre-Paul Sirven was legally rehabilitated. In the meantime Madame Sirven had died.

A more horrifying case to which Voltaire frequently refers though he was not himself involved in it is that of the Chevalier de la Barre. In August 1765 in Abbeville a crucifix on the Pont-Neuf was found to have been mutilated and another, in a churchyard, soiled. Suspicion fell on three young men, the Chevalier de la Barre, Gaillard d'Etallonde, and Moisnel. D'Etallonde escaped but the other two were arrested. The Chevalier de la Barre was only twenty years of age and Moisnel seventeen. Under torture Moisnel implicated a whole group of young men. They were all given suspended sentences except for the Chevalier de la Barre who was condemned for blasphemy. As Voltaire tells the story all that could be proved against him was that he had failed to kneel in the rain when a procession of Capuchins passed by, that he had sung and recited bawdy verses, and that he owned licentious books including Voltaire's pocket dictionary. His punishment was to have his tongue pulled out, his right hand cut off and to be thrown into the flames.

The same sentence was passed in absence on Gaillard d'Etallonde. He, however, had made his escape to Prussia, where he distinguished himself in the Prussian army. Voltaire took a continuing interest in his welfare and there are numerous references to him in the correspondence between Voltaire and d'Alembert.

Voltaire's *Traité sur la tolérance* was first published in 1763. It was reissued in 1766 together with *Le Philosophe ignorant*, one or two minor pieces condemning religious persecution in one form or another, and a notice to the public concerning the murders imputed to Calas and Sirven.

Le Philosophe ignorant adds nothing of importance to what we have seen to be Voltaire's views in an examination of the complete version of his philosophical dictionary. He again stresses our inability to penetrate the innermost secrets of nature, says of Aristotle and Descartes that they both begin by treating incredulity as the source of wisdom, with the result that they have taught him to believe nothing of what they tell him. As before, he is particularly severe on Descartes. This time he gives credit to William Collins as well as to Locke for talking sense about free will and rebukes Samuel Clarke for opposing them. He adheres to his view that all events are necessary, again uncritically bows down to the argument from design, and conceives of the matter created by the deity as being no less eternal than the deity himself, though he still shies away from Spinoza's identification of God with Nature. This time he ridicules the followers of Plato as well as those of Leibniz for supposing this to be the best of all possible worlds, and once again he avoids the difficult task of showing how his rejection of this doctrine can be brought into accord with his own affirmation that the course of nature, in every detail, is the necessary consequence of the decisions of a benevolent Creator.

After his sojourn in metaphysics Voltaire returns to Locke like the prodigal son to his father. He says that he agrees with Locke in holding that there are no innate ideas, that we cannot have an idea of an infinite space or an infinite number, or indeed any positive idea of the infinite, and that since one is not always thinking, thought is not a person's essence but an act of his understanding. He again subscribes to Locke's account of free will, to his theory of personal identity, and to his assumption of our incapacity to comprehend the nature of substance, and he again draws the inference that we have no grounds for supposing that God has withheld consciousness from matter, whether the matter be our own bodies or those of other animals.

His adherence to Locke, according to his own understanding, has left Voltaire with four or five truths, separated from a hundred errors, and burdened with a vast quantity of doubts. What he now wants from philosophy, unintentionally echoing Plato, is some answer to the question how we ought to live.

Here Voltaire parts company with Locke, dismissing as travellers' tales, unworthy of credence, Locke's examples of tribesmen whom it amuses to bury their children alive, and cannibals who castrate their sons in order to fatten them, and Mohammedan saints who couple with asses in order to avoid the sin of fornicating with women. Voltaire needs to discount such examples because he wishes to maintain that there is a law of morality that holds universally like Newton's law of gravitation, but his only reason for discounting them would appear to be suspicion of the motives from which the actions are said to proceed. He readily admits that Turkish sultans employ eunuchs to govern their harems and that boys are castrated in Italy for the preservation of their voices; he does not take cannibalism for a fiction, nor would he have needed to rely on the testimony of explorers to furnish examples of infanticide and bestiality. What is even more to the point, he could not have shown that those who engaged in such practices always thought them wrong. Surprisingly, he justifies the depradations of the brutal and licentious soldiery on the ground that these spoils of victory are the perquisites of their calling, adding that they would recoil in horror from the idea of murdering their sovereign or the members of his government at the inducement of even greater spoils. Instances of treachery, not only on the part of mercenaries, cast doubt on this historical judgement, but in any case the thesis that a soldier is morally entitled to treat any member of an enemy nation in any fashion that he pleases is not one that is commonly accepted.

Voltaire is at pains to show that all moralists from Zoroaster to Lord Shaftesbury, by way of the Brahmins, Confucius, the ancient Greek philosophers, Epicurus, the Stoics, even Hobbes, Spinoza and Bayle have been in fundamental agreement: they were all in favour of justice and virtue. This may very well be true, but amounts to nothing unless it can be shown that their conceptions of justice and virtue were the same and this appears not to have been the case. For instance Hobbes and Locke disagreed over the question of natural rights. More concretely, the proposition that some men are naturally slaves, which Aristotle accepted, did not commend itself to all later moralists.

Voltaire was not so inconsistent as to maintain that there were innate moral principles. What he believed was that just as the laws of nature were discoverable by properly conducted research, so a correct use of the understanding would unveil the true principles of morality. But here he runs the risk of getting into a circle. It looks as if the correctness of the use of our understanding is tested by the nature of the principles to which it conducts us. This is true in science also but scientific hypotheses are testable in a way that moral pronouncements are not, or at least not in any obvious fashion. I suspect that the test which Voltaire had in mind was that of general agreement, once prejudices had been overcome. Again there is the evident danger of circularity, since an appeal to its moral consequences may be involved in what is to be counted as a prejudice. The only way of escape that I can see is for the sources of prejudice simply to be listed.

To some extent this is how Voltaire proceeds. I do not know that he anywhere implies that religious prejudice is the only factor that clouds moral judgements, but he certainly took it to be the principal factor. This comes out clearly in his *Traité sur la tolérance*. The treatise begins with a reference to the Calas affair and then goes on to summarize the horrors for which religious fanaticism has been responsible throughout the centuries, especially in France. To show that one can safely refrain from insisting on religious conformity, he cites the current state of Germany, Holland, England and even Ireland. Going further afield, he adds Russia, Turkey, the state of Carolina, China and Japan. He has to admit that Catholics are debarred from public employment in England and pay double taxes, but in view of their support for the Stuart pretenders gives credit to English tolerance for the fact that they otherwise enjoy the general rights of citizens. The rulers of China and Japan did expel the Jesuit missionaries from their domains, but the Jesuits brought their fate upon themselves by their own displays of religious intolerance. The state of Carolina was picked out because it observed Locke's ruling that every head of a household of seven persons could impose on it any religion that he pleased, provided that all seven were in agreement. Voltaire would not have found it so easy to discuss the practice of religious tolerance in the puritanical states of New England. He conveniently forgot also that even Locke stopped short of the tolerance of atheism.

In general Voltaire is disposed to fasten the evils of religious intolerance wholly upon Judaism and Christianity. He acquits the Greeks, once more dismissing the counter-example of the fate of Socrates as a political aberration. He acquits the Romans, stressing the tolerance that they showed to Saint Paul, and dismissing as the fables that they undoubtedly are the tales of the penalties inflicted upon early Christian martyrs. In so far as the Christians suffered under Roman government, it was for civil not religious disobedience. It was left to the Christians, crucifix and bible in hand, to destroy one another's cities and shed one another's blood.

Is it to be wondered that there are atheists? No indeed, says Voltaire, but he will not admit that they are justified. They can point to the absurdity of Christian legends; to the murders of Huguenots by Catholics and of Catholics by Huguenots; to the use which has been made of confession, communion and all the sacrements to commit the most horrible crimes: it still does not follow that there is no God. On the contrary, he claims, anticipating an argument of Kant's, we should rather conclude that there is a God –

> who, after this passage of life, in which we have so greatly failed to recognize him and committed so many crimes in his name, will deign to grant us consolation for so much horrible misfortune; for considering the wars of Religion, the forty Papal schisms, which have almost all been bloody, the impostures which have almost all been harmful, the irreconcilable hatreds kindled by diverse opinions, in view of all the evils which a false zeal has produced, men have long suffered their hell in this life.

Of course, if men have made a hell of this life, it does not follow that God has a heaven prepared for them in a life to come. Even if we admit that there is a God, an architect of the universe, answering to Voltaire's conception, it does not follow that he intends men to be happy either in this or any other life; it does not follow that he plans a future life for them at all. This is surely not a point that escaped Voltaire. As we have already seen, he simply could not resolve the tension between his acceptance of the argument from design and his horror of cruelty and injustice, so much of which was ascribable to Christianity.

For modern tastes, too much of the *Traité sur la tolérance* is devoted to mockery of the Old Testament. It has to be remembered, however, that Voltaire was writing at a time when the orthodox view was still that this hotch-potch of Jewish history and faith was divinely inspired. He even finds it possible to credit the Jews with a measure of tolerance. The Saducees, who believed that our lives ceased with death, without any future punishments or rewards, the Pharisees who believed in fate and in reincarnation, the Essenes who believed that the souls of the good were dispatched to the Happy Isles and those of the wicked to a sort of Hell, all lived together if not in complete harmony, at least without persecuting one another.

Jesus Christ himself was not depicted as uniformly tolerant, but Voltaire makes light of such actions as the blighting of the fig tree, of such parables as that in which the King of Heaven is compared to a monarch who has a guest bound hand and foot and cast into outer darkness for failing to come to the celebration of the Prince's marriage in 'a wedding garment',[1] even of Jesus's saying 'If any man come to me, and hate not his father, and mother, and wife, and children, and brethren and sisters, yea, and his own life also, he cannot be my disciple.'[2] Like contemporary apologists for Christianity, Voltaire prefers to dwell on the passages in which Jesus is depicted as advocating kindness, patience and forgiveness. His object was not to serve the cause of any of the Christian sects but rather to weaken any claim which one or other of them might make that their savageries were authorized by the reputed words or deeds of Christ. His conclusion is that if you wish to resemble Jesus Christ you should be martyrs and not executioners, and he succeeds in compiling quite an impressive list of the pronouncements of religious authorities at various times against the use of force in the interests of religious conformity.

Voltaire, without further identifying them, refers to the members of a small Danish sect, who accepted the premiss that, whereas infants who die before being baptized are damned, those who die immediately after having received baptism enjoy eternal glory. They accordingly went around killing as many newly baptized infants as they could discover, thereby preserving them from sin, from the miseries of this life and from hell, and sending them infallibly to heaven. In the light of their beliefs they were acting rationally, but they did not secure Voltaire's approval. 'These charitable persons', he said, 'omitted to consider that it is not permissible to

[1]Matthew 22: 11–14.
[2]Luke 14: 26.

do a small evil as a means to great good; that they had no jurisdiction over the life of the children: that most fathers and mothers are sufficiently worldly to prefer having their sons and daughters with them than to see them slaughtered as a passport to Paradise, and in short, that the Law should punish murder, even when it is committed from a good motive.'

It follows that there should be limits to tolerance. Voltaire states his position succinctly:

> If a Government is to lack the right to punish men's mistakes, it is necessary that these mistakes shall not be crimes; they are criminals only when they disturb society: they disturb society so soon as they fall into the grip of fanaticism; consequently, if men are to deserve tolerance they must begin by not being fanatics.

It is plain from the context that what Voltaire is putting beyond the bounds of tolerance is religious fanaticism. His penchant for enlightened despots makes it uncertain whether he would go so far as Locke in according the right to civil disobedience. I have not discovered any theory of the social contract in his works. One point which is clear is that, granted the avoidance of religious fanaticism, he favoured much greater freedom of speech and particularly freedom of the press than was actually accorded either to himself or to his protégés, the *Encyclopédistes*. It is likely that he would have endorsed John Stuart Mill's principle that no limit should be set to anyone's freedom of expression except its impinging on the freedom of others. Notoriously, this leaves us with the problem of where this line is to be drawn.

There is, however, at least one passage in which Voltaire goes further than Mill. I believe that the final section of the *Traité sur la tolérance* is of sufficient interest and importance to be quoted in full:

> This essay on tolerance is a plea which humanity is very honestly addressing to power and to providence. I am sowing a seed which could one day yield a harvest. Let us all trust to time, to the goodness of the Sovereign, to the wisdom of his ministers, and to the spirit of reason which is beginning to shed light everywhere.

Nature says to mankind: 'I have caused you all to be born weak and ignorant, to vegetate for a few minutes upon the earth and to fertilize it with your corpses. Since you are weak, protect yourselves; since you are ignorant, achieve mutual enlightenment. When you are all of the same opinion, which will certainly never happen, then if there were only one man of a different opinion, you should forgive him; for it is I who cause him to think as he does. I have given you strength to cultivate the earth, and a little glimmer of reason to guide you: I have implanted in your hearts an element of compassion to enable you to assist one another in supporting life. Do not extinguish this element; do not corrupt it; learn that it is divine; and do not substitute wretched scholastic feuds for the voice of nature.'

'It is I alone who preserve your unity in spite of yourselves through your mutual needs, even in the midst of your cruel wars, so lightly undertaken, the eternal scene of misdeeds, hazards, and misfortunes. It is I alone within a nation who put a stop to the unhappy consequences of the interminable division between the Nobility and the Magistrature, between these two Bodies and that of the Clergy, between the townsman and the farmer. They all ignore the limits of their rights; but eventually in spite of themselves they listen to my voice which speaks to their hearts. I alone preserve equity in the courts, where but for me everything would give way to indecision and caprice, amid a confused heap of laws often passed haphazardly, or to suit a momentary need, differing from province to province and from city to city, and nearly always internally contradictory. I alone can inspire justice, where the laws yield only trickery; he who listens to me always judges aright; and he who tries only to reconcile contradictory opinions is the one who goes astray.'

'There is an immense edifice the formation of which I have laid with my own hands; it was solid and simple, everyone could enter it in safety; they wanted to decorate it with the strangest, coarsest and most useless ornaments; the building is collapsing on all sides; men are taking the stones and throwing them at each other's heads: I call out to them, Stop, get rid of this dreadful rubbish which is your work, and dwell with me in peace in the unshakable edifice which is mine.'

The voice of nature in this passage is the voice of reason. Voltaire's crucial assumption was that if men were rational they could live in harmony with one another. He can be accused of underestimating the conflicts of interest that set even rational men at odds. If it is only in Hume's special sense that reason can at all plausibly be said to be the slave of the passions, Voltaire went too far in the extent to which he accorded it the power of mastering them. In logic, his theory of the will should have taken him closer to Hume; but Voltaire was apt to forget his determinism when confronted with the spectacle of human cruelty and folly.

Voltaire is a great symbol. His name continues to stand for the homage to reason which is thought to have been distinctive of the intellectual outlook of the eighteenth century, especially in France. He and his disciples, like Denis Diderot and Jean d'Alembert, the standard-bearers of the Enlightenment, are contrasted with Jean-Jacques Rousseau who is regarded, especially by Lytton Strachey, as a predominant precursor of the Romantic movement of the early nineteenth century. After a meeting with Rousseau, Diderot described him as a madman and a damned soul. He wrote that the poets had been right in placing an immense interval between heaven and hell, implying that Rousseau resided in hell. Strachey's comment on this is that Diderot was wrong. 'The "intervalle immense", across which, so strangely and so horribly, he had caught glimpses of what he had never seen before, was not the abyss between heaven and hell, but between the old world and the new.'[1]

Is this a just estimation of Voltaire and Rousseau? I think that in Rousseau's case it comes at least very near to being so. It is true that there has been a widespread misunderstanding of Rousseau's political thought. The famous opening sentence of *Du Contrat social*, 'Man is born free but everywhere he is in chains', has been taken to imply that men ought not to be in chains, whereas in fact the principal aim of the book was to justify a particular form of political bondage, the subjection of the individual to the general will. Nevertheless Rousseau did put the legitimacy of all existing

[1]*Books and Characters*, p. 175.

governments in question. And his absorption in himself, carried eventually to the point of paranoia, was of a romantic character.

Voltaire, as we have seen, had a good opinion of his own talents and was not backward in pursuing his own advantage, but he was not an object of interest to himself, like Rousseau. A fair English comparison, also of eighteenth-century characters, would be that of Edward Gibbon with James Boswell. Neither was Voltaire much of a political reformer. He was mistrusted, in some degree persecuted, most of all by the French authorities, because he would not submit to their censorship, but the reason why he constantly risked falling foul of their censorship was not that his writings threatened the monarchy or even the privileges of the aristocracy but that they threatened the power and privileges of the Church. It is one of Voltaire's great merits that he was an uncompromising advocate of freedom of speech, but the form of this freedom which he primarily arrogated to himself was the freedom to expose, ridicule and denounce the past and current abuses of organized religion.

I have spoken of Diderot and d'Alembert as Voltaire's disciples. This is justified in the sense that they respected and deferred to him, but beyond sustaining their anti-clericalism, he hardly moulded their ideas. Whereas d'Alembert was pre-eminently a mathematician, Voltaire, apart from his seizing the opportunity to attack Maupertuis and his encouragement of the researches of Madame du Châtelet, took little interest in either mathematics or physics after the comparatively early publication of the *Lettres philosophiques*, not more than echoed by his subsequent *Éléments de la philosophie de Newton*. As we have seen, the theoretical content of the *Lettres philosophiques* was not original. Its main purpose and value was to import the theories of Locke and Newton into France and to break the stranglehold of Descartes over French philosophy and physics. It was more successful on the second count than on the first. It is only quite recently that British empiricism has begun to make some headway among French philosophers who have been surprisingly pervious to German metaphysics. Even in the domain of physics, the reign of Descartes was not quickly brought to an end. It was not, indeed, until the beginning of the nineteenth century that the authority of Laplace assured the supremacy in France of Newton's account of gravitation over Descartes's vortices.

As for Diderot, he was very much his own man. Though ably assisted by d'Alembert, it was he who devised and principally saw to the fulfilment of the plans of the *Encyclopédie*. Voltaire allowed himself to be enrolled as a contributor, but, as we have noted, his contributions were of minor importance. Diderot valued Voltaire as a patron, but apart from the anti-clericalism and the belief in free speech, which were common to all the apostles of the Enlightenment, there is no internal evidence that he was indebted to Voltaire for his own highly distinctive literary work.

To say this is not to disparage Voltaire. I think that it has to be conceded that *Candide* was his only literary masterpiece, but his writings cover an extraordinary range. If he was overrated in his own time as a poet and a dramatist, he has since been underrated as a historian. He was a master of satire and his voluminous correspondence is full of elegance and wit. His compliments to royalty, when not ironical, may sometimes appear high-flown, but his prose style was never pretentious, always concise, and beautifully adapted to its varied purposes. On this score alone he deserves the high place that he continues to occupy in the tradition of French literature.

This would not be sufficient, however, to account for the dominant role that he played in the French culture of his own time and the prestige that his name still carries, not only in France. There are various reasons for his contemporary dominance. He retained his vitality throughout what in those days was an exceptionally long life. He was a brilliant conversationalist as well as a gifted writer. His satire was merciless. It was also important that for the greater part of his life, he lived at a distance from Paris. This enabled him to obtain the aura of a living legend. His authority was all the greater through its being exercised from afar. But the most important factor, in my view, and the one that chiefly accounts for his survival as a symbol, is that he was fundamentally a man of action. More than any other writer he vindicated Robert Burton's commonly misquoted saying that the pen is more ferocious[1] than the sword.

How far was Voltaire successful in his campaign against 'l'infâme'? I find this question difficult to answer. I suppose that Voltaire bore some responsibility for the French Revolution, though a smaller share than Rousseau, and no doubt the French Revolution and the ideals of 'liberté, égalité, fraternité', which Napoleon's armies carried over Europe, weakened the political power of the Roman Catholic Church, but the most effective counter to the superstitions of Christianity came from the scientific discoveries of the nineteenth century. In this matter we owe a smaller debt to Voltaire than to such men as Lyell, Thomas Huxley and Charles Darwin.

In cases where it is wholly honest, the readiness of Anglican clergymen to accommodate their views to scientific thought has tended to lull English free-thinkers into the belief that there is no longer any need to worry about the abuses that provoked Voltaire's attacks. But this would be a parochial attitude. When we look farther afield and observe such things as the recrudescence of fundamentalism in the United States, the horrors of religious fanaticism in the Middle East, the appalling danger which the stubbornness of political intolerance presents to the whole world, we must surely conclude that we can still profit by the example of the lucidity, the acumen, the intellectual honesty and the moral courage of Voltaire.

[1]'Saevior' in the original Latin.

Index

INDEX

INDEX